CW00554476

COAST TO COAST

COAST TO COAST

Mike Parker

ISBN: 0-86381-898-6

This book is based upon the ITV1 Wales television series
produced by Cwmni Da.

Published by
Gwasg Carreg Gwalch,
12 Iard yr Orsaf, Llanrwst, Wales, LL26 0EH.
☎ 01492 642031   🖹 01492 641502
Printed and published in Wales.

This book is dedicated with love, respect and thanks
to the team who made Coast to Coast happen,
especially Emyr Jenkins,
Helen Williams-Ellis and Guto Williams.
Diolch o galon i chi gyd.

COAST TO COAST
CONTENTS

COAST TO COAST
INTRODUCTION

The call came as I was manoeuvring into a space in the supermarket car park. Series Producer Helen Williams-Ellis, of *that* family, was on the line on my little-used mobile phone. She wanted to know if I was interested in writing and presenting a six-part TV series voyaging around the Welsh coast in different boats. "Sounds great", I said, checking my shopping list to see if I'd remembered the tea bags. We chatted for ten minutes or so, and Helen promised she'd get back to me soon. I was pleased to be asked, obviously, but over a decade of freelance living had taught me that ideas, even the most apparently dead cert of ideas, don't always come to fruition, and it was best not to assume anything until the ink was drying on the contract. I plunged into the supermarket, more concerned with what might be the B.O.G.O.F. offer of the week than thoughts of boats and sea.

Helen sent me the proposal for *Coast to Coast* that had recently been submitted for commission to HTV Wales. It looked great, but there was one little nagging voice at the back of my mind urging caution. I am no sailor. My full previous boating experience consisted of a few trips on canal narrowboats in my native English Midlands, where the water is perfectly still, the speed limit a stately 4mph and there are pub stops every couple of miles. Much as I love looking at the sea, from the safety and solidity of dry land, the idea of being filmed trying to sail conjured up images of that daft bat from Cardiff learning to drive in front of the TV cameras and nearly killing herself and everyone else in the process. It could surely only end in tears, and they'd probably be mine.

Ever the diplomat, Helen batted down my fears that I was just not experienced enough as a sailor to cut it for *Coast to Coast*. "It's not a sailing series," she kept repeating. "The aim is to take a look at the land, at Wales, from the sea." Now that did interest me. A decade of writing about Wales, most regularly as the co-author of the *Rough Guide to Wales*, had given me a good basic knowledge of the whole country. There was no Welsh town of any size or import that I hadn't visited at least once, but my views of and about them were all from the land. How different would Cymru look from out there, beyond that "other" border? How much would I see that could only ever be experienced from the sea? What would the experience do for my understanding and opinions of Wales? The more I thought about it, the more excited I became.

So was born *Coast to Coast*. The first six journeys, taking us to all corners of Wales, were filmed between July and September 2002, finally hitting the small screen as a Sunday evening cheer-up-the-summer's-coming-back series in February and March 2003. The reaction was fantastic. I had been a mite nervous as to how people in Wales would take to the sometimes cheeky and opinionated views of their country from someone who hails from Kidderminster. And I'm sure there are people who would shout, "oh get bald English prat off quick" whenever *Coast to Coast* started. But everyone I met was hugely kind and enthusiastic. There is an honourable place in any culture for the perspective of an outsider, someone unencumbered with the same national baggage, and I was thrilled that so many people, of all ages and backgrounds, seemed to respond to my take on places.

They'd also responded, of course, to *Coast to Coast's* phenomenal photography, courtesy of our talented director-cameraman Emyr Jenkins. The eight hundred miles or so of the Welsh coast is a varied beast indeed, from the soaring cliffs of Ceredigion and Anglesey to the golden beaches of Meirionydd and the heavy industry of Flintshire and Glamorgan. Emyr managed to capture each and every mood of the coast, and his eye for the telling detail, whether an architectural flourish on a building or a movement of sunlight across cliff-top fields, never flagged. All the more remarkable when you consider the often hideous conditions that he had to put up with, particularly when trying to film the grandeur of the landscape from a boat rocking on choppy water in driving rain.

The second series of *Coast to Coast*, filmed in summer 2003 and broadcast in early 2004, enabled us more or less to finish the job of touring the Welsh coast. There were a few parts of the country – east Anglesey, south Pen Llŷn, southern Pembrokeshire, Carmarthenshire and Cardiff – that we, sadly, never managed to get round to, as the journeys would have been impossibly long, but within the twelve programmes, we managed to convey much of the variety and uniqueness of coastal Wales. Coastal communities are very much different from their inland counterparts. They have grown up entirely differently, with expansive horizons and influences culled from all around the world. It was repeatedly brought home to me just how comparatively recent the influence of land travel has been to these places, and it shows. Deliciously idiosyncratic and famously quirky, the coastal settlements of Wales are some its greatest assets. Combine the discovery of those with the utterly magnificent and often wild scenery that we were experiencing, and you can imagine what a lot of fun making the two series was for us all.

Just as the towns and villages of the coast were sparky and individualistic, so were the characters that we met inhabiting them. People who make their livelihood from the sea are a particularly single-minded bunch. They have to be. All else is secondary – family, career, relationships, houses – to the pull of the open ocean. Many people confessed that they couldn't stand staying inland, or even on land, too long. And, without exception, they were an amazing crowd to meet. Maybe it's the sense of perspective and mortality that a regular relationship with the sea engenders, but I've rarely met such calm, rooted people with such a balanced take on life – and death.

This book takes you on the twelve journeys that we made over those two summers, going anti-clockwise around the Welsh coast from Chester to Chepstow. It includes much of the stuff that made it into the final programmes, but also covers the stuff that didn't, more of my musings on the places we visited and some of the more entertaining behind-the-scenes scrapes that we found ourselves in. As well, of course, as some tangential ramblings around topics as diverse as golf, the shipping forecast, nudity, holiday homes, paganism, signposts and fairground vomiting. Writing this book has reminded me what a fantastic, Boys' Own adventure Coast to Coast was. If I think of just about anywhere on the Welsh coast, I can close my eyes and conjure up the image of how it looks from the sea. What a privilege. And what an experience – one that will live with me forever, and which produced some great telly of which I'm immensely proud. I hope you enjoy these tales from the stunning seaboard of this fantastic, fierce little country out on the rocky western shores of Europe.

MIKE PARKER
Esgairgeiliog, Powys
November 2003

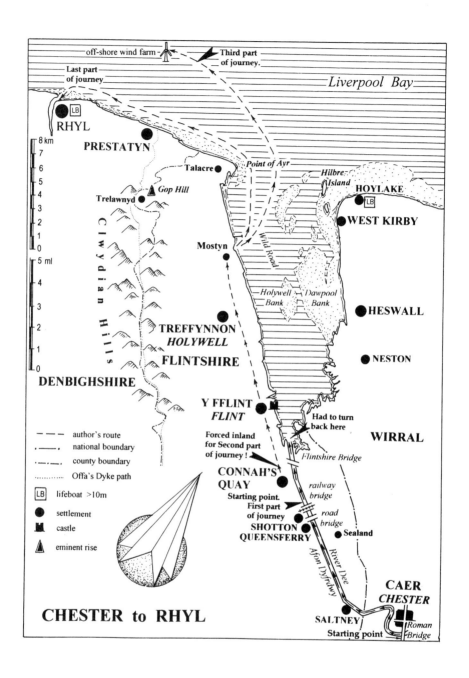

CHAPTER ONE:

CHESTER - RHYL

Border Terriers

This was the very last *Coast to Coast* that we filmed, in early September 2003. Yes, I know it's odd to start at the end, and odder still to kick off a book about the Welsh coast over the border in England, but bear with me. It will all make sense, I promise...

Chester is in England, but only just. Indeed, there is one Welsh village – Saltney – that has been swallowed by the sprawl and become a fully-fledged Chester suburb. The border slices through the south-eastern corner of the city, passing right down the middle of one Boundary Lane, of course. Wales on one side of the street, England on the other. It must get very noisy round there at international times.

From the Roman era, Chester has had a dual nationality as a frontier city between Wales and England. Skirmishes and fisticuffs have broken out regularly, as have laws to keep the two sides apart. One that's never been repealed dates back to 1403 and the time of Owain Glyndŵr's uprising. It states that "all Welsh people and Welsh sympathisers should be expelled from the city, and none should enter the city before sunrise or stay after sunset on pain of decapitation" – ironic really, when you consider that Chester is the place half of northeast Wales comes for a good night out and the chance to get, if not headless, at least pretty legless.

These factors, we felt, gave us every right to reclaim Chester as a Welsh city and start the programme there. It also gave us a chance to do some shopping. Chester is a city that has taken retail to a higher plane, and, to be honest, it's one that wrings me out and leaves me for dead after about an hour. The unavoidable tang of the city is one of cash, and lots of it. The city's evident wealth is shouted at every turn: shops calling themselves "purveyors of fine..." whatever, minimalist window displays, itsy-ditsy restaurants, well-heeled shoppers (and the flip side, innumerable beggars). It was to be a sharp contrast with the towns across the border.

Chester was a great medieval port, and it was the desperate desire to hang on to this status that caused the river Dee to be altered so massively in the early eighteenth century. The estuary was silting up at a rate of knots, making navigation as far as Chester hazardous and, all too often, impossible. A huge feat of engineering was conceived to canalise the river up to its tidal limit, building huge walls in the estuary and turning the river into a ruler-straight waterway. It didn't work as hoped, and the sands continued to move in, rendering the city impotent as a port.

In order to sail from Chester, therefore, we needed a boat with an extremely shallow draught and to hit high tide spot on. It was Connah's Quay fisherman Keith Marland who got us there. He rarely goes that far up the river these days, preferring to fish out in the more open waters downstream. Accompanying us on the journey was Dr Phill Barber, a local geomorphologist, whose knowledge of the Dee estuary and its strange history is second to none.

Bit of a squeeze: me, Dr Phill Barber, Emyr Jenkins (camera) and Dafydd Baines (sound) with Keith Marland on his boat up the canalised section of the Dee.

We left Chester at the amazing Roman Bridge, still in use for traffic after nearly two millennia. Just upstream is the famous city weir, of which there was only about a foot to be seen when we left, as we were on the cusp of high tide. During high spring tides, the weir disappears altogether.

From the river, Chester shows its smartest side. We passed the racecourse, built, as they frequently are, on the floodplain, and numerous palatial private houses at the top of raked and stepped gardens descending aristocratically to the river's edge. Not for the first time, I revelled in the secret views that boat travel affords. Having a property on the sea or a major river adds great bundles of noughts to its value, so you often find some of the grandest houses anywhere in such locations. From the road, they're usually all high gates, whirring cameras and security lights that snap on if so much as a leaf falls in the same postcode district. But from the river or sea, you can practically see what selection of breakfast cereals they've got in the kitchen. Marvellous. Parker by name, nosey git by nature.

Coming out of Chester, the river snakes and turns, before it enters the canalised section and crosses the border into Wales. The very first thing you see coming into Wales is the site of the old Crichton boatyard that was filled in and now houses one of those dispiritingly ugly, low-slung modern office blocks. Gathered round the entrance were a group of office employees having a crafty fag. That, apparently, is called progress. Croeso i Gymru.

Turning the last corner, we entered the dead straight section of the estuary as it skims across the flat plains of Flintshire. The river continues, without deviation or hesitation, for five and a half miles up to Connah's Quay. One common misconception about this stretch of water is that it acts as the Wales-England border. Indeed, it was intended to, just as the River Dee (and other rivers) provide the natural border elsewhere between the two countries. In fact, both sides are in Wales, the Welsh having managed to grab a two-mile corridor of land on the northern (English) side of the river. One explanation given is that there are many Welsh combatants from a border battle buried at the village of Sealand, on the northern bank, and it was felt that they should not have to spend the rest of eternity in England!

Before long, the industrial nature of the Dee estuary became the dominant feature. For hundreds of years, this stretch has been one of the most industrialised in Wales. I've got to confess that my preconceived image of it was stuck circa 1989, all battered heavy industry and rusty pools of water. Some of that remains – most notably in the terminally-threatened Corus steelworks at Shotton – but much has been swept away by hi-tech businesses and modern plants, each with the Welsh Development Agency logo plastered across them. I was gobsmacked by how much money was invested in this most north-eastern corner of Wales, riding high as it is on being so close to booming Cheshire, the Surrey of the North. It did strike me that, if north-eastern Wales and south-eastern Wales are doing so well, both thanks to their proximity to wealthier parts of England, then just how poorly is the rest of Wales? After all, when national statistics are evened up, Wales still always comes out worse than most other parts of the British Isles. Take the country's two genuinely wealthy regions out of the equation, and the rest of us must be in a pretty bad way.

I couldn't tell you where the towns of Connah's Quay, Shotton and Queensferry begin or end. I'm sure locally, there's a terrific sense of identity and fierce loyalty, but to an outsider, it all looks like one fairly indistinguishable sprawl strewn along the south side of the Dee. And not one, to be brutally honest, that you'd want to spend too much time getting to know. Dominating the towns are the mighty Corus steelworks, the splendid four-towered power station that elegantly punches the sky in an almost Soviet victory salute and, just as pleasing, the willowy arc of the new Flintshire Bridge.

Since the River Dee was canalised in 1737, getting across it has proved to be both a challenge and a major opportunity. Each new crossing has spawned developments clustered around it, from the ferries of the early days through the major Victorian road and rail bridges that gave an unprecedented boost to the growing towns of Connah's Quay, Shotton and Queensferry. The gleaming white Flintshire Bridge, opened just before the turn of the millennium, is the latest incarnation. With a central span of over 800 feet, the graceful arc glides high over the river, leaving room enough for ships to pass underneath. Traffic over the bridge is, shall we say, light at the moment, but with Europe's largest industrial park springing up next door, it's unlikely to stay that way.

Despite the thing going stratospherically over budget (how do we do that, every bloody time?), it is – fair's fair – a magnificent piece of engineering, and I hope it pays off. I was particularly impressed that the view towards it along the ruler-straight section of the Dee was absolutely perfect in its symmetry. The earlier three bridges at Queensferry all cross square on, and are pleasingly symmetrical. But to have ensured that the central A of the new bridge, which is beyond the first few turns of the river after the straight section and also crosses at a considerable diagonal angle, hits the exact same symmetry too is a masterstroke.

We were supposed to be docking at Mostyn, a few miles further up the estuary, but conditions worsened very swiftly. The speed the tide in the Dee estuary races in and out makes navigation difficult at the best of times. We were hitting a tide in full retreat at the same time that the wind had picked up. The consequence was beefy great waves chopping in the river, which we could do nothing but hit full on. As a result, we were all getting a thorough soaking, and Keith promised that it could only get worse. We wimped out, turned round and started to splash back to Connah's Quay. Unfortunately, Emyr the cameraman hadn't filmed my soakings and our decision to turn back, so we had to do it all again, just for the camera. You'll be pleased to hear that the elements played ball, and I got a thorough drenching. Again. Ironic really that the only section we had to abandon in all the Welsh coast was the upper reaches of a river!

So the next section of our journey had to be completed on land. First port of call was Flint. It's a name that has always struck me as an odd – and rather ugly – one. It conjures up an image of a place as hard as, well, flint – real hard, rock hard, don't mess. Flint was Edward I's new bridgehead into conquering north Wales, and it's thought that the name was chosen as the symbolic flint to light the spark which would consume by fire the War of Independence of Prince Llywelyn.

Contemplating the estuary from Flint Castle.

Flint was the first of Edward I's castles in northern Wales, and the first town built alongside it too. Like all the other towns built with his castles, Edward's Flint was an English-only enclave. The town's first charter of 1284 decreed that no Welshman was "allowed to hold civic office, carry weapons, hold assemblies or to purchase land or property in the borough", while the English settlers could "gather wood in the woods of the Welsh without payment". Three further charters over the next century made life even harder for the native Welsh, who – surprise, surprise – resented being treated so harshly in their own land. The burgesses of the borough sent a petition to the King in 1395 complaining about "the ill-will of the Welsh and their trouble-making and defiance of the law" – like a bunch of spoilt brat bullies whining to teacher when their victim finally hits back.

Today, aside from the castle, old Flint has pretty much been buried in a sea of sixties concrete. I know it must have seemed like a good idea at the time, but how the hell did people become persuaded that tower blocks and car parks were better than the original grid layout – like Conwy or

Caernarfon – that had managed so well for nearly seven hundred years? Determined not to be disheartened, I went to the library to see what fascinating facts I could find out about the place. I wasn't exactly spoiled for choice. Flint Town FC won the Welsh FA Cup in 1954. Ian Rush hails from here. And that was about it. Thank the Lord for football.

By the time the Dee reaches Flint, it has broadened out massively. It flares out even further as we headed north-west, the Wirral and Hilbre Island looming low on the horizon across the mudflats and glinting channels of speeding water. At this point, the estuary has, once again, become the national border, and you can't help but compare the two sides. The Wirral, on the English side, is where Scousers who've made a bit of cash move to. It's a land of big hairdos, bling-bling jewellery and gleaming 4x4s with bullbars and a tow bar for the boat. Flintshire, on the Welsh side, is altogether more humble in its aspirations.

Perhaps some of the humility seeps from the water supply. After all, the next town up the Dee is Holywell, which, on the signs as you enter it, declares itself to be "the Lourdes of Wales". It's been a place of pilgrimage for a thirteen hundred years, and many claim to have been healed by being dipped in the pool at the shrine. The natural spring feeding the pool was disrupted by mine working in 1917, and the water's been pumped in from the mains ever since, but – miracle of miracles – this hasn't stopped its healing powers. Or its earning powers, come to that. But Holywell doesn't come anywhere near Lourdes – or even somewhere like Knock in Ireland – in terms of the glutinous Catholic tat stakes. There's no stalls or shops nearby flogging Holy Mother biscuit tins or statuettes of weeping disciples ("Buy 11, get Judas FREE!"). I was deeply disappointed.

It was time to get back on the water. A couple of miles beyond Holywell is the strange little port of Mostyn, and we were due to catch our second boat there. I call Mostyn strange, because it was so unlike any of the other ports we visited doing *Coast to Coast*. It is the only privately-owned and run port in Britain, and that is the big difference. A management buyout, lead by Chief Executive Jim O'Toole, took the port over in the early 1990s. They undertook a huge restructuring and rebuilding of the place, the first substantial change since the eighteenth century. Against huge pressure from the big boys at Liverpool and Holyhead, Mostyn even managed, in 2001, to lure P&O into operating a daily ferry service to Dublin from there. When the wind farm was finally given the go ahead for offshore of Rhyl, it was Mostyn that adapted itself swiftly to cater for the construction and transport out to sea of the monster turbines. Mostyn has survived because it has always been able to change. Patricia O'Toole, Jim's wife, is a company director too, and Jim said to me that most of the big decisions about the port are taken at their breakfast table. There was something cheerfully Victorian and entrepreneurial about Mostyn and the O'Tooles, and such a contrast to the megacorps and their endless rules and regs that we encountered in every other major port.

The windfarm components at Mostyn Dock.

That said, we were treated at Mostyn to perhaps the most finger-wagging Health & Safety chat that we ever had to endure during the series. The wind farm construction site at Mostyn leases the land from the port, and is run by another set-up. With Jim O'Toole, we presented ourselves at the security portacabin. There was a lot of sucking in of cheeks and shaking of heads. We needed high visibility gear, helmets and protective boots, plus an address from the H&S officer, who came bustling over to us, clipboard tucked precisely under his arm, admonishing us for taking up his valuable time. Jim quietly sidemouthed to me "never trust a short man with a moustache". If this particular Health & Safety zealot was anything to go by, he's not wrong. This was your man's big moment. He'd got the boss of the whole port *and* a TV crew to nag, and he was in Health & Safety pedant's heaven. He went through everything, and I mean every possible potentially dangerous eventuality, in minute, spirit-crushing detail. I was trying hard not to catch anyone's eye, as I could feel a mild hysteria welling up inside me. It finally erupted out of me as a not-very-well stifled set of giggles when he said "now, fires on site. If you spot a fire anywhere in the controlled area, under no circumstances should you consider attempting to extinguish it." My giggles brought his withering gaze on me. "Do you have any problem with that?" he coolly enquired. "No, not at all," I replied, gulping for breath. "If I find a fire, believe me, I won't be trying to put it out". He glared at me, eyeball to eyeball, for the rest of the lengthy lecture. If he could have given me two hundred lines, he would.

We left Mostyn aboard the port's own boat, the *Fast Cat*, to go and take a closer look at the offshore wind farm north of Rhyl. The wind farm had been mooted for years as an idea, but it was only in early 2003 that construction was finally started on an initial thirty turbines five miles off the coast. We'd seen it, and heard about it, everywhere on this journey. It's an arresting sight, no more so than when we were filming top shots on the mountain above Prestatyn. It was a gorgeously clear day – Anglesey, the Isle of Man and even Blackpool could all be seen, and the wind farm looked almost touchable, it appeared so very near to the shore. At other times during the week of filming, just the tiniest drift of offshore haze and the turbines disappeared from view altogether. I'm not too sure whether I'd want them in my daily horizon, but the vast majority of people I spoke to locally were fully supportive of the project.

With us on the journey out to the wind farm was Pete Geddes, a PR man for National Wind Power, the farm's operators. Statistics trotted effortlessly off his tongue: each turbine was 400 feet tall, they will be able to power a town of 50,000 houses, the piles in which they sit are drilled more than sixty feet down into the seabed, and it's all part of meeting the government's target to produce 10 per cent of Britain's energy needs from renewable sources by 2010. The figure is around 2.5 per cent at present, so chances are these offshore wind farms are set to become a far more familiar sight. Drawing up close to the mighty turbines was, a mite disappointing. The ones in mid-construction on the quay at Mostyn looked bigger and more impressive than those already in situ at sea. It didn't help that, as soon as we neared the turbines, the heavens opened and it started to bucket down with rain.

Dropping Pete off back at Mostyn, we set off once again for a look at the final stretch of coast. All changed when we turned the corner at the Point of Ayr. The industry of Flintshire has its last flourish in the shape of the old colliery, the last pit in north Wales that closed in the 1990s, and, still working, the terminal where the gas from the Irish Sea fields is piped ashore. Just as the Point of Ayr is the last gasp of the industrial coast, so is it the beginning of the tourism coast. Talacre, the end-of-the-world little resort behind the Point of Ayr, is a small huddle of fun pubs and caravan parks sheltering behind the sand dunes that stretch all the way from here to Prestatyn, four miles west.

This section of coast gains more raised eyebrows and disparaging comments than any other in Wales. But, hand on heart, it was beautiful. The soft white dunes and big, wide beach backed by gnarled mountains gave it a real spacious grandeur that was recognisably, quintessentially

Welsh – something that I'd never felt about the coast up to the Point of Ayr. Buried deep in these hills is one very special peak, called the Gop, or Gop Hill, the second largest prehistoric artificial mound in Britain after Silbury Hill, near Avebury in Wiltshire. After so many reminders of the modern age along this stretch of coast, it was good to see that the mysteries of the ancient world still stand their ground here too. Unlike Silbury, which was built on a flat valley floor, the 46 foot mound of rubble on the Gop was built around 5000 years ago on top of an existing hill, itself over 800 feet above sea level. It's a powerful place, all the more so because we don't know exactly why our ancestors built it. It may have been a giant astronomical viewing platform, a centre for ritual, a monument to the dead or some great warrior's burial place (one persistent local rumour claims it to be Boudicca's final resting ground; at least it's not King Arthur, I suppose). Either way, it's a tremendous spot to view the coastline and the Clwyd Hills and to feel your connection way, way back through the generations. If you can't manage that, you could at least marvel at what must be Wales' very first slag heap.

Before long, the northern Wales resorts started with curiously disgruntled aplomb in the shape of Prestatyn. It's a low-key sort of place that largely eschews the glitzy seaside attractions of many of its rivals. You can have a round of crazy golf, a pot of tea, or walk along the long concrete prom, but it doesn't get a lot more heart-racing than that. When we were there, it was Sunday afternoon, and we did manage to find a troupe of line dancers clacking their way round a pub car park in the town centre. I've never been a huge fan of line dancing, considering it to be dancing for folk who can't really dance, but this crowd's enthusiasm was infectious, and we passed a very enjoyable hour or so with them, and they surely gave it their best for the camera.

These days, a fair proportion of visitors to Prestatyn are Offa's Dyke Path walkers, for the town's beach, just by the Nova Centre, is where the path either starts or stops, depending on which way round you're doing it. If you started at the other end, near Chepstow, to wade into the sea at Prestatyn is the traditional way to finish the hike. After 177 miles of gorgeous borderland scenery, all winding rivers, ancient woods and luscious hills, I can't help but think that this finale in downtown Prestatyn could only be described as something of an anti-climax. Perhaps best start here instead.

And so to Rhyl. Writing the *Rough Guide to Wales* has given me a strange relationship with the place, largely because the book was so rude about it. It was my co-author, Paul Whitfield, who wrote the town's account in the first two editions, starting it with the immortal words

"Anything you can do in Rhyl, you can do better elsewhere". Every time the book came out, the great and the good of Rhyl rose up in indignant horror and demanded a retraction and grovelling apology. For the third edition of the book, Paul and I swapped areas of Wales, meaning that I'd update the areas he'd previously covered and vice versa. Doing the research, I breezed into Rhyl and made for the tourist office. When I announced what I was doing there to the Bwrdd Croeso lady behind the counter, she reached immediately for her phone and punched out an internal number, without ever taking her eyes off me. "Come down quick," she barked into the receiver. "The bloke from the Rough Guide's here."

Within seconds, a man galloped down into the office and withdrew me to a quiet corner, where he made an impassioned plea for me to improve our opinion of Rhyl. After spending a day or so in the town, I had to agree that the *Rough Guide* account did verge on a rather haughty snobbery, and I rewrote it from scratch. Having a go at Rhyl is like scoring a goal from five yards when the goalie's already left the pitch. It's just too damn easy. Rhyl never has been, and never will be, a sophisticated resort, but it does what it does with great gusto and good heart, and is as good a place as any for a cheap, cheerful seaside blowout. Personally, I'd hate to see all British resorts become trendy surf hang-outs or full of pretentious wine bars. Somewhere like Rhyl makes you marvel at the ways we Brits like to have fun.

We're a versatile family, as can be seen in Rhyl (pic M.P.)

And it is fun. When we arrived on the prom, I plunged happily into the arcades, followed in hot pursuit by the crew. After an hour or so of bingo, plastic horse-racing, tuppenny falls machines, attempts at claw-grabbing teddy bears and pinball, I was sated, slightly poorer and the proud possessor of a stuffed Scooby Doo toy that I'd won for my legendarily speedy wrist action on the Kentucky Derby horse race. Does life get much better than that?

Chester and Rhyl. So near, and yet so very, very far apart. It had been a journey of extremes, but a memorable one all the same. This is the part of Wales that probably feels less Welsh than any other, but there's still a real national pride here. Nowhere in Wales will you find more passionate fans of the Welsh football team, even if rugby and Cardiff-based institutions like the National Assembly leave people hereabouts colder than a dip in the Rhyl briny. The Alyn and Deeside consituency, centred on Connah's Quay and Buckley, recorded the lowest turnout amongst many dismal others for the 2003 Assembly elections, when fewer than one in four voters could even be arsed to go to the polling station. Even in better political times, I suspect enthusiasm up here for all-Wales institutions, most based hours and hours away in Cardiff, will never be sky high. With Chester, Manchester and Liverpool just a Gucci shoe's throw away, who'd feel connected to Cardiff? Come to that, chances are no-one in this area ever saw *Coast to Coast* anyway – they're all tuned in to Granada. Their loss!

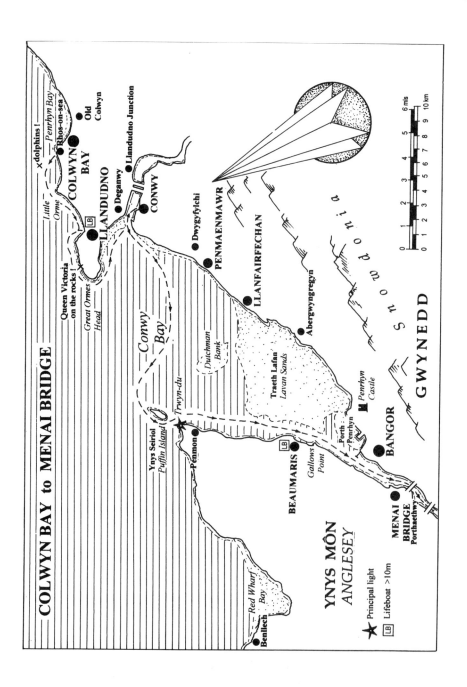

COLWYN BAY to MENAI BRIDGE

YNYS MÔN
ANGLESEY

★ Principal light
LB Lifeboat >10m

Benllech
Red Wharf Bay

MENAI BRIDGE
Porthaethwy

BEAUMARIS

Penmon

Ynys Seiriol
Puffin Island

Trwyn-du

Gallows Point

Porth Penrhyn

Penrhyn Castle

BANGOR

GWYNEDD

Traeth Lafan
Lavan Sands

Duchman Bank

Abergwyngregyn

LLANFAIRFECHAN

PENMAENMAWR

Dwygyfylchi

Conwy Bay

Great Ormes Head

Queen Victoria
on the rocks!

Little Orme

LLANDUDNO

CONWY

Deganwy

Llandudno Junction

COLWYN BAY

Rhos-on-sea
× dolphins!

Penrhyn Bay

Old Colwyn

Snowdonia

0 1 2 3 4 5 6 7 8 9 10 km
0 1 2 3 4 5 6 mls

22

CHAPTER TWO:

COLWYN BAY - MENAI BRIDGE

Lassie Come Home

This episode of *Coast to Coast* was screened in the first series, and many people told me that it was their favourite of that first batch. It became one of mine too, mainly for the sheer variety of things that we saw along the way, and the good laugh that we had filming it. It's a hugely diverse piece of coastline, one that you could happily explore for months.

We kicked off in Colwyn Bay, and tried to think of the most appropriate place to open the programme. In many minds, Colwyn Bay is synonymous with genteel B&Bs, places popularly believed to be stuck in about 1958. We scoured the town for such an establishment and came up with a wonderful example, all ruched curtains, flock wallpaper and porcelain figurines. It made Derek the Weatherman look butch. The idea was that the beginning of the programme would have me asleep in the guest house and dreaming of some of the weird and wondrous things to come on the journey ahead. We arrived at the B&B at three o'clock on a baking hot summer's afternoon to film the bit of me waking up in bed and then having breakfast. I stayed chatting with the proprietors while Emyr, the cameraman and director and Dafydd, the sound man, went upstairs and set up in one of the bedrooms. Following them up a few minutes later, I was greeted with the sight of a small suburban bedroom filled with wiring, lighting, camera and microphone. It looked for all the world as if we were filming a low budget porn flick. That was bizarre enough, but having to tuck into a full bacon and eggs bonanza at 4pm on a boiling summer's day was even more surreal.

Although there's a sea view from its uppermost edges, Colwyn Bay doesn't look or feel much like a seaside town. The beach is out of sight and out of mind as you walk its tired streets. This town centre is down on its luck and you can't help but feel sorry for it. To get to the seafront, you have to duck down below the A55 dual carriageway, before bursting out the other side on the prom. Centrepiece here is the Victorian pier, one of many that we were set to encounter on this journey. In many ways, the pier is a metaphor for the town itself. There are glorious touches of rampant Victoriana, coupled with a few dashes of post-war modernism, but it's all in desperate need of a lick of paint and some serious TLC. In summer 2003, the pier was sold privately, after the owner had failed to flog it on an internet auction site, so here's hoping the new owners take their new toy seriously.

There's no harbour or jetty at Colwyn Bay, so it was a short walk up to Rhos-on-Sea to rendezvous with our boat for the journey west towards Anglesey. Rhos is Colwyn Bay's posher neighbour, a cluster of antique shops and tearooms that lulls you into easy strolling. It almost feels like a fishing village, but it isn't; the harbour here was built purely for pleasure boats. And moored just beyond the defensive wall, I caught my first glimpse of *Lassie*, our boat for the journey. Love at first sight.

Lassie is a sixty-five year old breed of vessel known as a Conwy Nobbie, also known as Morecambe Bay Prawners. These were specially-adapted yachts that began to appear in the late nineteenth century, shallow of base and nippy across the water. After a long working career, *Lassie* is now enjoying her well-earned retirement – appropriate then that our journey to take us along north Wales' famous Costa Geriatrica. Our skipper was Scott Metcalfe, the Bangor-based specialist in wooden shipbuilding, who'd restored the *Lassie*. With us were Doug Smith, the boat's ebullient owner, his partner Carol and son Giles.

From the sea, the first striking thing to notice was just how developed the coastal strip is here. Prestatyn, Rhyl, Kinmel Bay, Towyn, Abergele, Llanddulas, Colwyn Bay and Rhos-on-Sea all merge into one another in a seamless, uninterrupted sprawl, some sixteen miles long. It was something of a relief to see nature reassert itself as we approached the headland of the Little Orme. This ancient limestone crag, and its bigger brother the Great Orme, perfectly frame the seaside resort of Llandudno that we could just see peeping around the corner. But there was an unexpected diversion in the shape of a school of dolphins playing out at sea. Scott turned us round and we headed off to see them.

Words cannot do justice to the experience of having a load of dolphins showing off around you. They were jumping either side of the boat and evidently playing with us, and loving every single second. It was quite breathtaking. There really is something about these graceful creatures. I'm as cynical as anyone, but after a few minutes of this, it was all I could do to stop myself stripping off, leaping in and having the proverbial mystical experience. After the dolphins had moved on, we started to steer back towards Llandudno, all of us with daft, soppy grins spread across our faces.

Being serenaded by dolphins off the Little Orme.

Every travel writer who's ever visited Llandudno has come away at least reasonably impressed by the unity and scale of the town's Regency architecture. Even Bill Bryson, in his often hilarious *Notes from a Small Island*, took a break from his all too predictable pops at the northern Wales coastline to admit that Llandudno was "truly a fine and handsome place". It's even better from a boat. Instead of approaching the town past B&Q superstores and miles of thirties semis, and then spending forty minutes driving around in circles looking for a parking space, all of which kind of dilutes the impact of the place, we just rounded a corner and – bang! – there it was, laid out like an elegant Merchant Ivory film set. My instant reaction was of the stark contrast with Colwyn Bay, which hides from its own seafront. None of that malarkey with Llandudno. The whole town drapes itself with unabashed pride around the gentle curve of the bay, sandwiched with perfect precision between the dual hummocks of the Ormes, Great and Little.

If the resorts of northern Wales were a family, Prestatyn would be a quite likeable, but rather dull, cousin, Rhyl a beered-up brother who you worry might be nicking cars and Colwyn Bay the ageing auntie who lost her looks years back. But the biggest character in the clan is Great Uncle Llandudno, the elegant old chap who might be a bit threadbare in places if you look a little too closely, but who can still swagger with a certain bygone panache. From his position spread languidly around the bay beneath the Great Orme, Great Uncle Llandudno looks along – and it has to be said, looks down on – the rest of his family with a barely disguised shudder of horror.

We picked up the cheerful and very knowledgeable local historian, Tom Parry, to give us a few further insights into the town. He told me that, prior to 1850, the town was little more than a few simple single-storey turf houses sheltering under the Great Orme on an open salt marsh. It was down to Edward Mostyn, the local MP, who pushed an Enclosure Act through Parliament, granting the exclusive rights to develop the land into a sophisticated resort to – go on, guess – one Edward Mostyn MP. They don't change, do they? Llandudno is still basically owned by the Mostyn estates, and it is that singularity of ownership, coupled with the fact that most of the town sprang up almost instantaneously in one short period, that has kept the place so unified visually.

Tom accompanied us on a voyage around the Great Orme, towering 680 feet above the town and one of the topographical wonders of Wales. It's a complete world apart from the effete charms down below. Wild goats and sheep roam its fields, one of which has become a kind of open-air drystone graffiti park, where people have written their names or favourite footy teams from the plentiful supply of loose limestone boulders. Well, it sure beats a marker pen in the bus stop. The Orme, its rocks 300 million years old and full of precious minerals, feels as if it's been barely tamed by man, although the Victorians, as ever, had a good go. Marine Drive, the toll road that circumnavigates the Orme, was hacked out of the rocks and opened in 1878. Tom told me that Prime Minister William Gladstone came to visit, and, thanks to his chronic vertigo, had to be blindfolded and led around by a local.

The Victorian flavour of both Llandudno and the Great Orme reached a dazzling zenith when we reached the far side of the headland, just

Her Majesty is on the rocks! 'Queen Victoria' on the Great Orme

below the famous castellated lighthouse. The rocks from the lighthouse down to the sea are said to resemble the shape of Queen Victoria's head, a phenomenon that can only be seen from the sea. Now, I'm usually pretty sceptical about these kinds of optical illusions, but this one is a blinder. It really does look like the outline of Her Majesty's bonce, and, to cap it all (quite literally), the crenellations of the lighthouse fit perfectly as a crown on top. I could only imagine the excitement of the first person to notice the resemblance, as he galloped into town exclaiming "I have seen Her Majesty in the rocks!" Llandudno would have felt very blessed.

She-who-was-not-amused was not the only optical apparition that Tom pointed out around the Great Orme. Almost as soon as we'd passed Llandudno's elegant pier, he picked out a cave in the side of the cliff. This is *Yr Ogof yr Hanner Dydd*, or the Cave of Mid-Day (it sounds so much better yn Gymraeg), so named because at midday on the two equinoxes (Spring and Autumn, when the day and the night are of exactly equal length), and only at this time, the sun's rays pierce the cave and illuminate the back wall. Slightly less significant, but fun all the same, he also pointed out the Frog Cave, which really does look the face of a grinning, wide-mouthed frog!

The water became distinctly choppy around the far side of the Orme, and I wasn't too unhappy to turn back to Llandudno, ready for an evening out. During the day, the town does live up to its reputation as the capital of blue rinses and afternoon teas, but, by night, it's an entirely different beast altogether. The average age on the streets drops by about half a century, as the swabbed and scrubbed youngsters of northern Wales hunt in packs around the town's numerous bars and clubs. It's Ibiza with thermal undies on.

Centre of the action is Upper Mostyn Street and its legion of trendy watering holes. I'd wanted to film a piece to camera about the phenomenon, so we set up on a warm Friday evening, from about half past nine. Camera crews and youngsters fuelled on Bacardi Breezers are not a great combination. It took hours, mainly because a succession of girls, most of them wearing little more than a few stray strips of material, tottered over for some impromptu careers advice "'cos I really wanna be on the telly, like". Groups of drunken lads, by contrast, mainly acknowledged our presence by showing us their arses. I was beginning to feel like someone's dad. It was definitely time for bed.

The following day, we rejoined the *Lassie* to continue west to Anglesey. The resorts of northern Wales retreated into the distance as we headed for a much wilder, much Welsher section of coast. First port of call was Conwy. Doug, the owner of the *Lassie*, became quietly sentimental as we cruised up the estuary of Afon Conwy into the town, for this, of course, was the birthplace of the boat, one of a breed known as a Conwy Nobbie. She was built, Doug told me, in 1937 right by the harbour wall. It was good to see a fair few other Nobbies bobbing up and down in the Marina. The Conwy River Festival had just finished, and many of them had returned, like salmon, to their spawning ground for the occasion.

As happened so often in the making of *Coast to Coast*, Conwy presented an entirely different face from the water to the one that I was used to seeing on land. The monumental castle and town walls all angle themselves to the water's edge, and it wasn't difficult to imagine a great flotilla of medieval traders' ships jostling for position at the quayside.

Conwy was always an important, and notorious, staging post on the difficult land journey across northern Wales. Only a decade or so ago, all traffic had to crawl at snail's pace through the tight little grid of streets, before the A55 tunnel under the town was completed. The freeing up of the town has had enormous benefits, not least a far better chance to admire the three bridges that cross Afon Conwy below the castle. They're all for different forms of transport and date from different ages (the original Thomas Telford suspension bridge of 1826, now for pedestrians only, the tubular railway crossing of 1848 and the "new" road bridge, completed in 1958), but they all have one major thing in common, and that's that they take their visual cue from the turrets and battlements of the castle and town walls. It's a wonderful example of combining pizzazz with practicality.

There's a lot more to the town than the castle and the bridges. Within Conwy's thirteenth century walls, there are over 200 listed buildings from every architectural age. Best of all is the utterly gorgeous Plas Mawr, the finest Elizabethan town house to be found anywhere, complete with its fantastically scatological and gory displays about Elizabethan health and hygiene. Right at the other end of the spectrum is that popular oddity on the quayside, the self-declared "Smallest House in Britain", whose two tiny rooms, one above the other, measure a total of nine foot by six. The house's last inhabitant was a 6 foot 3 fisherman, presumably with a large permanent bump on his forehead.

Back on the *Lassie*, we had to head out from the shore as we continued towards Anglesey. Beneath the sea is a huge sandbank, called the Traeth Lafan, which, prior to the opening of Thomas Telford's Menai Bridge across to Anglesey in 1826, was the main route over to the Beaumaris ferry. People would have to cross at low tide, using local guides who knew how to pick their way across the sands, avoiding sinkholes and water channels. Not surprisingly, it was a hazardous crossing and many were caught out by racing tides and sudden surprises.

It didn't matter that we couldn't hug the shore so closely at this point. So dramatic is the stretch to the west of Conwy, stepping back a bit actually gave us a better perspective. Here the foothills of the Carneddau range of mountains (the second highest in Wales after Yr Wyddfa, Snowdon) tumble straight down to the water's edge, hemming all human activity into one pencil-thin coastal strip of land. Quite what man has managed to pack into that strip is amazing. The settlements of Dwygyfylchi, Penmaenmawr, Llanfairfechan and Abergwyngregyn fight for space with the mainline railway and the new A55 expressway. As well as their own town signposts, presumably. With the quarried out mountainsides backing them, it made for an awesome sight.

The Lassie
*rounding Puffin
Island*

We were aimed squarely at Puffin Island, that little teardrop of land off Anglesey's eastern edge. Like most offshore lumps of rock around Wales, Puffin Island is a holy place. Its Welsh name, Ynys Seiriol, remembers the Celtic saint who set up his monastic cell here in the sixth century. Nowadays the island is uninhabited by man but has a thriving wildlife. Puffins are back, after being decimated by both rats and locals who thought that pickled puffin was the ultimate savoury snack – no, really. As we sailed gently around the island, my mind was far from the birds, as my attention was drawn to a colony of doe-eyed seals basking on the rocks in the gorgeous evening sunlight. Like the dolphins, seals seem to elicit a deep-rooted response that you have almost no control over. In their case it was one of chuckling admiration and perhaps even a tinge of envy. Lying there, lapping up the velvet summer's evening, they looked as chilled and relaxed as it's possible to be. That's what I want to come back as.

Rounding Puffin Island and then sliding quietly past the stiff sentryman of Penmon Point lighthouse, we had our first good look at Ynys Môn, or Anglesey. And then it happened. The moment that will live with me forever as one of the definitive *Coast to Coast* memories. Across the Menai Strait, the cotton wool clouds over the peaks of Snowdonia were gently tinged with radiant hues of apricot, pink and gold, as the evening melted into night-time. Hand on heart, I have never seen anything so lusciously beautiful. The eight of us on the boat – the four TV bods and the four boat crew – all fell into reverential silence as we tried to eat the scene with our hungry eyes. No-one spoke for a couple of minutes, and amongst a gaggle of telly people, believe me, that's a first.

Darkness was really beginning to fall as we chugged, by now back under motor, up the Strait. We were behind schedule, but, as ever, the sea is no respecter of schedules or timetables, and we just had to go with it. Time was really marching on though, and we were all ravenously hungry. With an hour's journey still left before docking at Porthaethwy, Menai Bridge, a ripple of panic passed round that we probably wouldn't be on land before 9.30, and that the great pub dinner we were all dreaming about could well shrivel into three pints apiece and a bag of nuts. It's not often that I say this, but thank heavens for mobile phones. Someone phoned the Liverpool Arms in Menai Bridge, and they promised to keep serving food until we arrived. We finally made it through their doors almost an hour after their normal shut-off point for food, but, true to their word, they dished up nothing short of a feast to eight starving, sunburned, snivellingly grateful desperadoes. And no, we never did the "but we're a TV crew" routine to get better service, just in case you're wondering. They're just nice to everyone. But that will be a free steak and chips next time, please.

The following morning looked grim. The wind had picked up, rain was squalling intermittently, but we plodded on regardless and sailed back up the Menai Strait to film the parts that it had been too dark to see the night before. I was getting soaked as I tried to mug off-the-cuff pieces to camera about what we could see. Half way through talking about Beaumaris castle, I was walloped by a wall of water. By now, there was a force seven blowing – technically, a gale – and we were pitching and rolling worse than the youth of Llandudno had been the night before last.

That wet, weary journey at least gave us the chance to tick off the third and fourth piers on my list. Strange, but true, but this one trip along the Welsh coast contained more seaside piers (Colwyn Bay, Llandudno, Beaumaris and Bangor) than you'll find in all the rest of Wales (this was an ongoing topic of discussion for days, and we never managed to come up with any more than Penarth, Mumbles and Aberystwyth elsewhere, so do feel free to prove us wrong). The oddest of them all has got to be Bangor. It's tucked away right at the back end of town, and it just kind of wanders aimlessly for a few hundred yards out into the Menai Strait. There's no arcades or cafes or any of the other usual trappings of a pier – just lots of wrought iron over a mudflat and a stiff breeze. All very bracing.

The pier is Bangor's most obvious feature from the sea – indeed, you can see surprisingly little else of the city. The Penrhyn estate has grabbed most of the available seafront hereabouts, both for its own port, Porth Penrhyn, and the vulgar ostentation of Penrhyn Castle. Our skipper, Scott Metcalfe, is based at Porth Penrhyn and we visited him there in his workshop where he fits out wooden boats to order. He's got no time whatsoever for the plastic tubs that you see in most modern marinas. Like many of the people I met during *Coast to Coast,* Scott is a purist and something of an obsessive. You've got to be for this sea life.

At Porth Penrhyn, a commemorative plaque celebrates its building as a result of the profits of the slate trade. The Pennant family of Penrhyn owned all of the slate quarries in this area, notably the huge tracts around Bethesda, just down the road. Their considerable wealth was, however, garnered mainly from sugar plantations that they owned and ran with an iron rod in the West Indies. It did strike me that it would be all too easy – and all too appropriate – to change the first T in "slate trade" on the plaque to a V.

The Pennants' wealth has come from lousy sources. Their vile practices in Jamaica set them up for bringing the harshest conditions possible back home with them. Workers at their northern Wales quarries experienced some of the worst of it, culminating in the famous three year long strike at the turn of the twentieth century. While their workers struggled in poverty and atrocious work and living conditions, the Pennants were busy building for themselves the three hundred roomed Penrhyn Castle, a monstrous memorial to megalomania that still seems to give off an air of stuff-you arrogance.

By the time we limped, drenched and depressed, back into Menai Bridge, it was time to call it a day. The weather was worsening by the minute and there was no improvement forecast before the next day. All that we could do was retreat to our hotel and spend the rest of the day trying to warm up in the sauna and jacuzzi. Tough life eh? Fortunately, the next day dawned glorious, and it was back down to the water to complete the journey along the Menai Strait in the company of Terry Beggs, a former Merchant Navy officer who lives overlooking the Strait and who'd spent the last few years photographing the many moods of this infamous, and often dangerous, channel of water. Terry is a local photographer who'd illustrated a marvellous recent book about the Menai, written by the eminent Gwyn Parri-Huws, who sadly died on Christmas Eve 2003.

The Menai Strait is an enigma – in Welsh, it's called Afon – or river – Menai, and although it often looks like a gentle river, it is, in fact, open sea with a fierce five metre tidal range. Small wonder that it took two of the greatest engineers in history – Thomas Telford and Robert Stephenson – to span the gap with their monumental bridges. All part of the Menai's heroic character. (I have to own up to getting this bit of the programme, when it was broadcast, badly wrong in that I attributed the second Menai crossing to Isambard Kingdom Brunel. Even if I'd checked with my own book, the *Rough Guide*, I'd have managed to steer clear of such a daft cock-up, one that, incidentally, brought the greatest number of phone calls to the duty desk at HTV. Those viewers are sharp cookies, and I can only own up that it was all my fault, and I'll never forget who designed that bridge again. It is now etched in my brain.)

Terry guided us through a notorious section of the Menai, known as the Swellies or Swillies. Despite sounding like a new set of brightly coloured blobs on kids' TV, they are, in fact, a razor sharp reef of rocks just underneath the swirling currents between the two bridges. We had to hit the stretch spot on with the tide, and, even then, the water was bubbling and frothing as if it was boiling. Small wonder that many vessels, lulled into a very false sense of security by the bucolic surroundings of the Menai's two banks, have come to grief here. The most famous casualty was the four thousand ton Naval school ship, *HMS Conway*, which floundered in the 1950s when it was being towed up the Strait. A towrope snapped, and the glorious old boat drifted on to some rocks and broke up. One of its last batch of cadets was one Iain Duncan Smith, who later in life very nearly did much the same thing to the Conservative Party.

The Menai Strait was a fine finale to the journey. It has, as Terry said to me, "so many changing moods that you never tire of it". His work has taken him all over the world, and it is always to the Menai that he returns, claiming it to be the finest sight on the planet. I'd learned a huge amount on this trip. To be honest, out of all the journeys that we did in the first series, this had been the one that I'd been looking forward to the least. I'd assumed it would be a tatty ragbag of dull old resorts and little more. But I was wrong, for it was on this trip that I saw some of the most ravishing views that Wales has to offer, and that's saying something. So will I learn the lesson not to be so snotty about places and pre-judge them quite so severely? No, probably not.

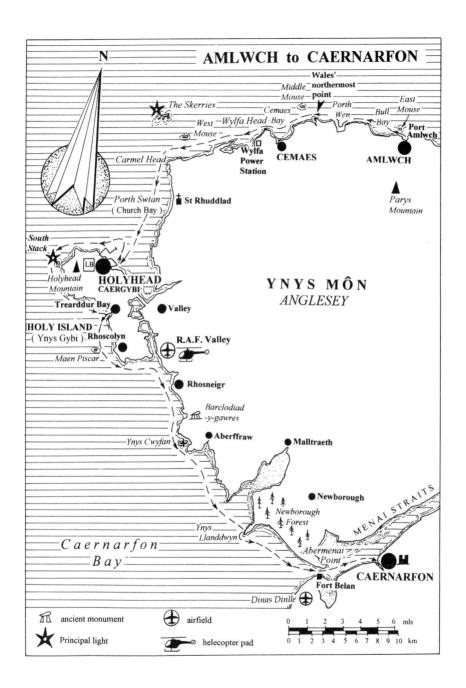

AMLWCH to CAERNARFON

N

Wales' northermost point
Middle Mouse
The Skerries
Cemaes
West Mouse
Wylfa Head-Bay
Porth Wen
East Mouse
Bull Bay
Port Amlwch

Carmel Head

Wylfa Power Station

CEMAES

AMLWCH

Porth Swtan (Church Bay)

✝ St Rhuddlad

▲ Parys Mountain

South Stack

Holyhead Mountain

LB

HOLYHEAD
CAERGYBI

YNYS MÔN
ANGLESEY

Trearddur Bay

● Valley

HOLY ISLAND
(Ynys Gybi) **Rhoscolyn**

Maen Piscar

R.A.F. Valley

● Rhosneigr

Barclodiad -y-gawres

Ynys Cwyfan

● Aberffraw

● Malltraeth

● Newborough

Newborough Forest

Ynys Llanddwyn

M E N A I   S T R A I T S

Abermenai Point

C a e r n a r f o n
B a y

CAERNARFON

Fort Belan

Dinas Dinlle

🛕 ancient monument

⊕ airfield

★ Principal light

helecopter pad

0 1 2 3 4 5 6 mls

0 1 2 3 4 5 6 7 8 9 10 km

CHAPTER THREE:

AMLWCH - CAERNARFON

The Isle of Mam

And so to Anglesey proper. After flirting with the island in the first series, a year later it was time to fling back the duvet and leap on in. I've always loved Ynys Môn. Partly, it's the island thing. Connected it may be to the mainland, but it makes not one jot of difference to the stubborn, we'll-do-it-our-way-thankyou flavour of the place. Then there's the spectacular change in landscape that occurs as you cross the Menai Strait, from the savage peaks of Snowdonia to a rolling, pastoral landscape that makes for such a refreshing difference. I've often heard it said by people that Anglesey looks dull, but then discovered that this impression only came from crossing the island on the old A5 route to Holyhead, through dusty little villages clogged with lorries and caravans heading to and from Ireland. Well, yes, from that angle, the island doesn't show its best side. But that's a major part of the appeal. I love places where you have to dig a bit to find their hidden nuggets. Anglesey has many: the greatest concentration of prehistoric sites in Wales and some of the country's finest beaches for starters. To travel three-quarters of the way round the island's coast was something I was greatly looking forward to. And it fulfilled every hope and expectation.

We had decided to start the journey in Amlwch Port, on the island's north-eastern corner. Amlwch is one of the oddest towns in all of Wales. It's sheer remoteness and bizarre history give it at atmosphere like no other. A tiny fishing village until the mid eighteenth century, it exploded suddenly into life, swiftly becoming the second biggest town in Wales and with a reputation for working hard and playing even harder. With literally hundreds of alehouses, plus a few breweries and tobacco plants, Amlwch was a raging, lawless boomtown, more in keeping with the Gold Rush settlements of America than rural Wales. And it was all thanks to copper.

To get a take on Amlwch, you need to go to Parys Mountain, a mile or two south of the town and the source of its coppery wealth. Television crews cannot resist the lure of Parys, for it is one of the most visually bizarre landscapes in the country. We were no exception, and decided to start the programme on the mountain's ravaged, pocked slopes. Many commentators have likened Parys Mountain to a technicolour moonscape. It's an apt image when you consider that the island of Anglesey itself is something of a distant satellite to Planet Wales, and that many Welsh folk, particularly those down south, are almost as likely to go to the moon as they are ever to come here.

The surreal landscape of Parys Mountain.

Copper has been mined on Parys Mountain for thousands of years. But it was the last copper age, starting in the mid eighteenth century, that took the industry onto another level altogether. Thousands of miners chipped away at the mountain's fabric, tunnelling deep into its sides and leaving spoil heaps and sulphuric pools in their wake. Emyr, the cameraman, had never previously been to Parys Mountain, and he fair skipped around it, so excited was he by the sheer visual possibilities it offered. Every corner you turn, there's some new and bizarre sight: rocks of impossible hues, the ruined windmill on its peak, the contrast between the ravaged slopes and the velveteen green fields around it.

Amlwch's boom came because it was noticed that the cast iron hulls of boats in the port seemed to be immune to rusting, thanks to the high copper content of the water. Demand for this protection soared, although the glory days were over by 1820, when falling world prices and technological difficulties caused by water seepage into the workings combined to spell the beginning of the end. The port today, where we were leaving from, is a sad shell of a place. All too often, there's a feeling in some Welsh communities of a hugely important past, but it's coupled with a distinctly uncertain present and an even vaguer future. Small wonder that we tend to cling like barnacles to the hull of history. But when, as in Amlwch, a town's heyday was not even in living memory, but two whole centuries ago, the palpable lack of a present or future is even more poignant than usual.

There are grand plans afoot (aren't there always?) to restore the port to its Georgian heyday, and, to that end, Amlwch Port made an impassioned plea for funds from the voting British public in the BBC2 heritage-meets-*Big Brother* series *Restoration*. It was eliminated at the first hurdle, so now trustees are looking to lottery money, Objective One cash and so on. Whether the best idea for the future is faithfully and painstakingly to recreate the past is, in my opinion, a moot point indeed.

Once again, it was to Scott Metcalfe, the wooden boat-builder of Bangor, that we turned for a vessel. *Vilma* was a gorgeous wooden 1920s schooner that Scott had faithfully restored. We left Amlwch with local historian Brian Hope, who further illuminated the town's bold and brilliant history. From the sea, Amlwch presents a very downbeat face, dominated as it is by the huge chemical works that extracts and processes bromide from the sea. I'd always thought that bromide – that secret ingredient in soldiers' tea that was supposed to prevent them from becoming too frisky – was as much a relic of the past as chastity belts, but evidently not. But then I've not hung round many barracks lately.

Near the entrance to Amlwch port is the easternmost of three small islands. In English, they're named the East, Middle and West Mouse, thanks to a supposed similarity to mice in their shape. I couldn't really see it myself. In Welsh, the East Mouse is known rather more prosaically as Ynys Amlwch. The Mice, despite their sweet-sounding name, have, over the years, been responsible for many a devastating shipwreck and much loss of life.

The first stretch of coast was spectacular, a riot of cliffs and coves speckled with intriguing remains of times gone by. Only a couple of miles west of Amlwch, Porth Wen was a glorious sight. A natural scoop of sea out of the land, it includes a beautiful (and deserted) beach and the dramatic ruins of a brickworks that has all the grandeur and gravitas of an old cathedral. The speciality of the place used to be producing yellow bricks, although the road to the end of that particular rainbow had come to an abrupt halt, and looked a lost cause. It may not even have much of a future as a gaunt old ruin, Brian told me. The sea, he said, is undercutting the old works from below and they won't last much longer.

From here, the cliffs became even higher, climbing to the peak of land at Porth Llanlleiana. Apart from the offshore bump of the Middle Mouse, this is the northernmost point of Wales, and a fearsome, dramatic place it is to hold such a title. Just at the moment that I was contemplating this in a dreamy reverie, the brooding bulk of Wylfa nuclear power station appeared around the corner and shattered the moment with blunt abruptness. It was sited on the Anglesey coast as it needed a staggering 53 million gallons of water for cooling purposes *every hour*. When it was built in the late 1960s, Wylfa was the largest nuclear plant in the world. Its construction also spawned a good ghost story. During the excavation of a tunnel, workmen regularly saw a ghostly female figure dressed in white drifting by, often humming or singing. It later transpired that the station was built where a house named Galan Ddu had once stood, its last resident an opera singer Rosina Buckman, whose ashes were buried in a box that was disturbed during the construction work.

I had my own slightly spooky experience hereabouts a couple of years ago. I was spending a very enjoyable, and leisurely, ten days or so exploring Anglesey on *Rough Guide* duty in my old camper van, now sadly despatched to that great scrap yard in the sky. As I was bumbling around the island, I heard on the news and saw in the local papers a story about someone who'd nicked a car and ended up torching it at Cemaes Bay, that pretty little port village near Wylfa. One night I decided to park up on the outskirts of Cemaes. It was late October, and night was falling early, so I finally pulled into a large, deserted car park after darkness and settled down for the evening. I let the dog out, and she scampered around happily enough, but, after a while, I noticed that the carpet on the floor of the van was becoming blackened and filthy. Thinking nothing particularly of it, I settled down for a night's sleep, which was disturbed by some really odd dreams. One that particularly remained in my memory involved me being sent to court and then to prison for a crime that was never specified. I can still remember the sense of absolute frustration as I tried to prove my innocence to all and sundry, but to no avail. Next morning, I woke up and saw where I'd been spending the night for the first time in daylight. Without knowing it, and with the whole vast car park to choose from, I'd managed to place the van slap bang over the scorched, burnt patch where the stolen car had, just a few days earlier, been set alight. I was absolutely, as snooker commentators put it, inch perfect.

Before long, we were approaching Anglesey's top left corner, Trwyn y

Gader or Carmel Head. A few miles out at sea, the rocky islets of The Skerries hunkered down on the horizon, dominated by their lighthouse. What a bleak posting that would have been in its day. On the headland itself are the remains of one of the dozen or so semaphore stations that punctuate the Môn coast, built in the nineteenth century as a way of quickly alerting the port of Liverpool to an impending ship.

Once we'd turned the corner around Carmel Head, the massive breakwater of Holyhead loomed into distant view. Before reaching the port, we passed some wonderful beaches, each backed with cliffs that contain some of the world's oldest rock, known as Pre-Cambrian and over a thousand million years old.

Coming into Holyhead, a huge white liner was berthed at the edge of the port. This was a US cruise ship, with seven hundred wealthy Americans on board. Apparently, every day that they go on land throughout their cruise, they spend on average a staggering £100,000 in the local area. I've got a horrible feeling that, while they were on Anglesey, most of that hundred grand would have gone into the tills of the bloody awful sweater shop at Llanfair PG. It really is the worst tourist attraction in Wales, and that's amongst some mighty stiff competition. The long name, a nineteenth century fabrication, is mildly interesting, but, once you've photographed the sign, all there is to do is admire the coaches in the oversized car park and get ripped off mercilessly in the tacky tourism outlets clustered around it. Does anyone ever go there twice?

Size, we're assured, really doesn't matter, but no-one seems to have told the port of Holyhead. Two rival companies operate the ferry route between here and Dublin, one aboard what they boast to be the "world's largest car ferry". Not to be outdone, the other company operate what they call the "world's highest car ferry". Boys, boys, boys, calm down.

But you can't help but get drawn into all the bragging. Everything

The Port of Holyhead.

38

about the place is massive, having been built out over both Salt Island and reclaimed land, allowing huge, and often rapid, expansion. The operation is no less impressive, especially when the vast ferries dock and disgorge their cargo with just minutes separating them. It's a far cry from the early days. The original 1821 custom house, now the staff club, sits forgotten and forlorn on the old quay, next to the arch that was erected at the same time as a ceremonial flourish to mark the end of the A5, an echo of its beginning at Marble Arch in London.

After the sheer scale and superlative claims of Holyhead the port, it's only a couple of hundred yards to Holyhead the town, though it might as well be a good few light years away. In 1727, Jonathan Swift described the place as "scurvy, ill-provided and comfortless", and no-one's had much better to say about it since.

The port's booming success, great though it is for Holyhead, only throws the town's perpetual struggle with poverty and isolation into even starker relief. There are bold plans afoot to re-unite port and town to a far greater extent, and you have to hope that they bear fruit. Otherwise, the best that can be said is that there's some lovely coast and countryside nearby, and, failing that, Dublin's only two hours away. Oh, and the scurvy seems to have cleared up pretty well.

The sad truth is that, like most ports, Holyhead is not a place to linger, but somewhere to get out of as swiftly as possible, and no amount of well-intentioned plans from Anglesey County Council, the National Assembly or the EU will change that. But there's also a more nebulous reason for the town's permanently down-at-heel atmosphere. At least with Fishguard, there's some sort of parity between it and the port at the Irish end of the operation, namely Rosslare. Both are moderately attractive small towns, with comparable status and amenities. Poor Holyhead, however, is on to a loser being placed opposite Dublin, that roaring, booming, million-strong capital of the Celtic Tiger. It only makes Holyhead look even poorer and even more ragged than it already is.

Holyhead won the unofficial *Coast to Coast* award as, without question, the most difficult town in which to film in either series. It was a bloody nightmare. And that's partly down, I suspect, to the fact that TV crews are a real rarity here. Most people assumed we were filming some piece of grim local news for *HTV Today*, and word spread mighty fast that we were around. Trying to film a piece to camera walking down the main shopping street proved nigh on impossible. People would just run at the camera, pulling faces, shouting "Hello Mum!", swearing and all of the other deeply predictable responses. And that was the adults. You can only begin to imagine what the kids were like. It was such a contrast to places like Caernarfon, Rhyl, Swansea or Aberystwyth, where people are used to seeing TV crews and thus left us to get on with it. It took us almost two hours to get a few lines recorded successfully, and – being the highly-strung creative types – we were all pretty stressed by the end of it. I feel daft enough as it is wandering down streets chatting to a distant camera, but trying to do it when people are really playing up makes me want to disappear into the cracks in the pavements. It's times like that I wonder how "real" TV presenters do it. And why.

Someone in Holyhead once said to me that the reason the town is such a crazy place is because it's on an island, off another island, off another island, i.e. Holy Island (Ynys Gybi), off Anglesey, off Britain. It makes some kind of warped sense. After all, the strange nature of island inhabitants has often been noted, and Holyhead sure does feel remote, even with the new A55 expressway halving the journey time across to Bangor and comparative civilisation.

If that observation is true, then the old lighthouse keeper at South Stack, around Holy Island from Holyhead, must have been a complete fruitcake, for it's on a further island still. Nowadays, over four hundred steps down the cliff lead to a bridge over the churning waves, but for the first few decades after the lighthouse was built in 1809, the keeper had to reach his little rock by virtue of a rope pulley system across the chasm. That is what you call dedication to duty.

South Stack and Holyhead, just a couple of miles apart, sum up the wide differences of Holy Island. At one and the same time, it contains the very best, and the very worst, of Anglesey. Away from its main town, the island is spectacular, a patchwork of scattered settlements, beautiful beaches, ancient remains and mesmerising cliffs. More than anywhere else in Wales, it reminds me of the best of the west of Ireland. We moored in Trearddur Bay, four or five miles beyond South Stack and took the rib into the shore, with the express purpose of taking a look at an archaeological dig taking place right by the beach. Numerous sixth or seventh century graves have been found here, although little is known about quite why there's such a concentration of them at this point. The site is dedicated to the great Celtic fire goddess, who became St Bride or Santes Ffraid in Welsh (hence all the villages called Llansantffraid something or other), otherwise known as Bridgit in Ireland.

After a few hours in Trearddur Bay, I really did feel as if I'd gone back in time – if not to the sixth century, then at least to the 1950s. There's something very Enid Blyton about the place, with its pristine beach, rocky setting and determinedly old-fashioned amenities. It's not difficult to see the appeal, and it's no surprise that Trearddur is somewhere that people return to for their holidays year after year after year.

Back on the *Vilma*, we continued around the heartbreakingly beautiful coast of Holy Island, past the scattered settlement of Rhoscolyn and its couple of lovely coves. Just beyond, the island ends and we were back to looking at Anglesey, Ynys Môn proper. First sight was the enormous RAF Valley airfield, built in the second world war over one of the holiest of Welsh lakes. Anglesey was the capital of the Celtic druidic tradition, and Llyn Cerrig Bach, when it was drained to build the runway, was found to contain over a hundred ancient artefacts, including ritual tools and precious ornaments. Nowadays, RAF Valley is the place where many of the ear-blistering fighter jets that roar over north and mid Wales originate. Quite what it must be like for the residents and visitors of Rhosneigr, slap next door, is hard to imagine. If Trearddur Bay is the holiday resort for those who want to head back to the 1950s, Rhosneigr seems designed for those who'd prefer to pretend that the Edwardian age hadn't yet ended.

More reminders of Anglesey's ancient and sacred past flashed by. First up, it was just possible to spot the bump on the cliff tops that is Barclodiad-y-Gawres, or the Giantess' Apron, a heavily restored 5000 year old burial chamber. Deep within the chamber are some stunning original patterns carved into the walls, most notably the chevrons and zigzags that show great similarity to those found across the water at Newgrange in Ireland, one of the most awesome neolithic sites to be found anywhere.

A mile or two further on, the amazing sight of St Cwyfan's church gradually loomed into view. The thick-set little building, sitting on a circular walled island lapped by the tides, dates back to the seventh century, but it is highly likely that the site was a holy spot before the Christian church adopted it as one of their own. A circular churchyard – and St Cwyfan's is as near perfect as possible in that regard – is a fairly common indicator of a pagan site that was taken over by the Christians, and there are numerous examples throughout Wales. It's a commonly understood fact that many Christian and Western festivals – e.g. Christmas, Easter, Hallowe'en/All Saints' Day, May Day – have deeply pagan origins and are still infused with much pagan imagery and symbolism. So it is with the landscape. Paganism is, after all, an earth-based belief system, so it stands to reason that practitioners would have been able to locate the most important, or charged, parts of the earth and made them their special places of worship, gathering or burial. On the coming of Christianity, many of these charged places were appropriated wholesale and had churches built upon them. Aside from any spiritual or magical aspect, keeping the familiar places would have made the gentle (and often far-from-gentle) coaxing of people from paganism to the new

Church much easier.

Immediately after St Cwyfan's church and island, the coastal landscape changed once again. Rocks and reefs gave way to spectacular, dune-backed sandy beaches, places that, even in the middle of the hottest August on record, were near deserted. The first expanse of sand was the lovely Traeth Mawr at Aberffraw, for centuries the seat of the Gwynedd princes. Next up came Malltraeth Sands and then the beaches fringing the vast conifer plantation of Newborough Forest, either side of the quite magnificent Ynys Llanddwyn, Llanddwyn Island. With the growing backdrop of the mountains of Eryri, it all looked impossibly romantic and beguiling. Appropriately so, because Llanddwyn is the celebrated Welsh capital of love.

For it was here that Santes Dwynwen retired to live the life of a nun, heartbroken after the breaking off of her affair with the Gwynedd prince Maelon sixteen centuries ago. God forbid that our patron saint of all matters of the heart should have had a happy love life, ooh no. Much better that she suffered in lonely solitude all her days with just the cormorants for company. Just how Welsh is that?

Mind you, it's given Anglesey the chance to market itself as the Welsh Capri – that's the island, not the car. A couple of years back, Anglesey county council launched a marketing campaign to capitalise on the romantic credentials of the island, rebranding itself under the quite brilliant title of "Anglesey – Ynys Môn Amour." Well, who'd want a loved-up weekend in Paris or Venice when you could share a bag of chips in Holyhead?

Sarky quibbles aside, Llanddwyn Island – although only really an island when there's a very high tide – is enough to make anyone start feeling gooey. It is truly one of the most glittering jewels of the Welsh coast, where soft beaches, romantic ruins and distant mountains are all washed in an ethereal, blue light. For various reasons, we had to leave the shooting of the section on land at Llanddwyn to the very final day of filming, and it was the most delightful place to bring *Coast to Coast* to an end. It was one of the few places we visited that I'd never actually been to before, although I'd wanted to for years. The weather was perfect and it didn't disappoint at all. Quite the contrary – I can't wait to get back there.

On the boat, we were now nearing our destination at Caernarfon. Navigating through the sand bars that mark the entry to the Menai Strait is notoriously difficult, so we were joined by Caernarfon pilot Richard Jones to steer us in. Richard is a lovely bloke, and, amazingly, is the seventh generation of pilots in his family. Talk about career pressure! He says, though, that his dad didn't actually want him to go to sea, and neither did his dad before him. Richard went away to college to study electronics, but the call of the sea soon became too loud to ignore and he was back doing what his family had done so well for centuries.

The narrowest point of the Strait is at its entrance, where the rock and sand bank of Abermenai Point, on the Anglesey side, almost touches Fort Belan, a Napoleonic fortress that guards the mainland side. The Fort is in the family of the Lords of Newborough, and Richard told me a particularly entertaining story of one of the more recent title-holders. In the 1970s, the then Lord Newborough fired one of the Fort's cannons rather carelessly. The wadding from the cannon went straight through the sail of a passing yacht, for which his lordship was hauled up in front of the local magistrates and fined.

A different perspective: Caernarfon and its castle from the water

Once through the gap, Caernarfon loomed large into view. Many times on these journeys, the perspective from the sea has completely changed the way that I've seen a town, and this was one of the best examples. On land, I've never been a particularly huge fan of Caernarfon castle – "that most magnificent badge of our subjection", as Thomas Pennant so eloquently put it. It always seemed so big and brutish, not somewhere that invited a flicker of romance or mystery. How different it looks from the sea. With the purple and grey peaks of Snowdonia hunkering down behind, the castle looks out over the water with calm self-assurance, invoking wonder and terror all in the same moment. Of course, almost every rebel who's ever tried to have a tilt at the castle or town would have arrived by sea, and it's obvious that when Edward I brought in the world's foremost castle-builder, James of St George, to get it built, the critical viewing angle was the one that I was now getting for the first time. Like so many other things that I saw during the making of *Coast to Coast*, it will be etched on my memory until I cough my last.

Some Welsh towns and districts, despite having been battered by waves of attempted homogenisation over centuries, have a granite uniqueness stamped through their core like lettering in a stick of seaside rock. You can smell it in the air. Caernarfon is a case in point. All the more remarkable, though, for this is a place whose seed was firmly planted in the soils of oppressors – firstly the Romans, and subsequently the English king Edward I and the British monarchy. Half a billion television viewers around the globe watched the 1969 Investiture of the heir to the English throne as the Prince of Wales in Caernarfon's clenched fist of a castle. "A Royal Town" announce the signs on arrival to the coachloads of visitors who pour in to follow his steps. But if tourists come expecting a Welsh Windsor, all cream teas and pot pourri, they are in for one hell of a shock. Despite its flawless imperialist pedigree, Caernarfon is raw, republican, and fiercely, passionately Welsh.

(Covis Dre) Caernarfon (pic Dewi Glyn Jones)

I hooked up for a chat with brilliant local photographer, Dewi Glyn Jones, to help explain the whole Cofi thing. Cofis are Caernarfon people, born and bred, and Cofi is the name given to the version of Welsh that is ubiquitously spoken here, one that even other Welsh speakers find difficult at times. Dewi had to admit that he wasn't a proper Cofi, having

44

only moved to the town at the age of one! "To be a real clansman of a Cofi, you have to born within the town walls to begin with," he said, "so I'm a bit of an adopted Cofi really." He talked a lot of clans and tribes, for Caernarfon always has been – and remains to this day – the meeting and market place for the tribes and clans that live in the rugged little mountain villages all around.

Caernarfon's brusque individuality was a fitting end to a journey around one of the most gloriously stubborn parts of Wales. With the sad exception of Holyhead, the entire journey had been so beautiful, it would make anyone want to cuddle up to this amazing coastline. But you get the feeling that if you cwtch this area too tightly, chances are it'll bite back. All the more reason for loving it, and treating it with the respect it deserves.

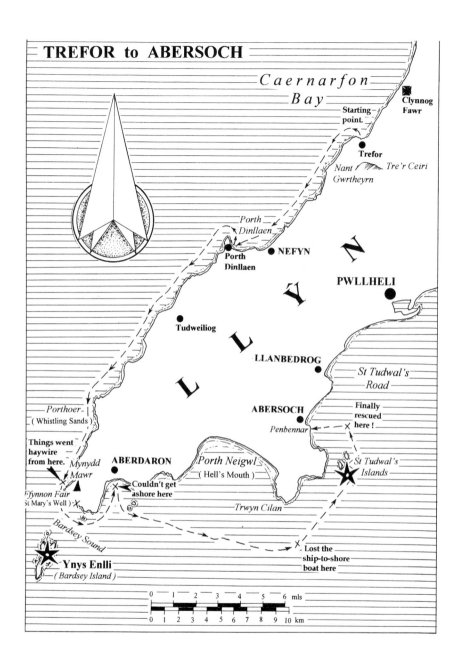

TREFOR to ABERSOCH

Caernarfon Bay

Clynnog Fawr

Starting point.

Trefor

Nant Gwrtheyrn — Tre'r Ceiri

Porth Dinllaen

Porth Dinllaen

● NEFYN

LLYN

PWLLHELI ●

Tudweiliog ●

LLANBEDROG ●

St Tudwal's Road

Porthoer (Whistling Sands)

ABERSOCH ●

Penbennar

Finally rescued here !

Things went haywire from here. Mynydd Mawr

ABERDARON ●

Porth Neigwl (Hell's Mouth)

St Tudwal's Islands

Couldn't get ashore here

Ffynnon Fair (St Mary's Well)

Trwyn Cilan

Lost the ship-to-shore boat here

Bardsey Sound

Ynys Enlli (Bardsey Island)

```
0   1   2   3   4   5   6 mls
0 1 2 3 4 5 6 7 8 9 10 km
```

CHAPTER FOUR:

TREFOR - ABERDARON
(well, Abersoch actually)
from Heaven to Hell

The final programme of the first series was also the last one we filmed in the summer of 2002. For many people, especially my friends, it was the one that made them laugh the most, largely thanks to the fact that we got into real trouble towards the end of the journey and the terror is all too evident on my face.

It all started so promisingly, though. Llŷn is an amazing part of the world. The finger of Welsh coast pointing at Ireland drips with a power and passion that has long been expunged in so many other places. Its comparative isolation, beyond the natural barrier of the Snowdonia mountains, has kept Llŷn as a fortress of *Cymreictod*. All too often, this is portrayed merely in linguistic terms, for Llŷn is certainly one of the most steadfast bastions of the Welsh language. But it's so much more than that. The language may be the mortar that holds the bricks of Llŷn society together, but the bricks themselves – the rural patchwork of farms and villages, of *plas* and *bwthyn*, the glorious and unspoilt coastline, the civility and kindness of the people – are just as beguiling.

Pilgrimage was a major theme of this programme. Ynys Enlli, the "island of the currents" or Bardsey as it is known in English, sits at the tip of Pen Llŷn, and is Wales' most holy spot. We were following the northern coast of the peninsula, itself a major historical pilgrims' route down to Enlli. It seemed appropriate to start the journey at the massive St Beuno's church in Clynnog Fawr, the most impressive and celebrated of the many pilgrims' churches that dot this coastline. It's a curious old mix of spartan, monastic touches such as the whitewashed walls and flagstone floors, together with more ornamental flourishes and little indications of considerable medieval wealth, courtesy of the pilgrims that passed this way and halted awhile.

To further augment the spiritual fortification, we climbed one of my favourite peaks in Wales, Tre'r Ceiri, or the Town of Giants, just outside the village of Llanaelhaearn. The climb itself is impressive enough, with your eyes constantly drawn to the rounded, breast-like hill next door, Mynydd Carnguwch. With its perky cairn providing a perfect nipple, no surprise that it is known locally, and with a typically Gog deadpan sense of humour, as *Broneneth* or Carn Tit.

Tre'r Ceiri is the best-preserved Iron Age hillfort in Britain. The fortress is surrounded by giant stone walls, fifteen feet thick in places and once through them, you're surrounded by the circular remains of dozens of dwellings, all over 2000 years old. They were originally occupied only through the summer months, making Tre'r Ceiri the very first Llŷn holiday park, way before even Butlin's at Pwllheli got in on the act. It's a haunting, bracing spot with stunning views over the whole of the Llŷn. Hundreds of feet below, we could see what looked like the toytown village and harbour of Trefor, where we were due to catch our boat.

If there's one defining feature of Trefor, it has to be its Welshness. Over 90% of the population speak English only as a second language, and, even then, have very few occasions where they would ever need to. The village, which has starred as a film set for an S4C soap opera, is both pretty and gritty, dwarfed as it is by the old granite quarry that reminds me, in my more fanciful moments, of an Inca temple. In its heyday, Trefor quarry employed a thousand people, and it's a real testament to the resilience of the village that, since its semi-permanent closure, the strength of the community has survived – and even thrived.

Although it's in a fantastic location, the harbour at Trefor is never likely to become a trendy marina, thank God, as its moorings are owned and controlled by the villagers themselves. Our boat was owned by Llŷn farmer Ifan Davies and we were joined by Geraint Jones, former headmaster of the local school, leader of the famous Trefor Brass Band and founder member in the early 1960s of Cymdeithas yr Iaith, the Welsh Language Society.

Once out of the shelter of the harbour it soon became apparent that the sea was a lot rougher than it looked from land. The sky was an obstinate porridge grey and there was a fair wind whistling too. By now, it was the second week of September. There was a definite autumn nip in the air. My mind turned nervously to the journey ahead. If it was this rough already, how bad would it get in Bardsey Sound, that notorious two mile stretch that separates Ynys Enlli from the mainland? It's supposedly the roughest piece of sea on the whole of the British coast. Gulp.

As we were chatting on the harbour wall before boarding the boat, Geraint Jones said to me how he was rather nervous of trying to string sentences together in English for the camera. "I haven't spoken it for months," he confessed. It proved to be a groundless fear. Geraint is eloquent and erudite in any language, and his informed, lively commentary was one of the highlights of the whole series for me. He is a man who knows his patch intimately and was able to marshal facts, figures, anecdote and opinion together with a deftness of touch.

With Geraint Jones of Trefor on the boat

The first misconception he blew apart for me was about the name of his home village. I'd assumed that Trefor was a gluing together of Tre'r Fôr, the town of the sea. Not a bit of it. It was named after one Trefor Jones, the first quarry manager of the mighty granite quarries that sit brooding above the village. Before long, we were passing some stupendous cliffs – the best in all of Wales, said Geraint, which was apparently something that Wynford Vaughan Thomas had once stated. They were certainly menacing and impressive. A mile or so from Trefor, we came to a deep cleft scored in the cliffs, some forty feet high and only four feet wide. "This is the Welsh Acapulco," Geraint said with evident pride. Apparently, Trefor boys (including Geraint in his youth) swim round the coast to this spot, climb to the top of the cleft and then hurl themselves down through it and into the sea. It looked terrifying, but I was jealous all the same. The Kidderminster equivalent of daring from my teenage years was managing to get through one of the underpasses without being offered a bag of glue to sniff.

Nant Gwrtheyrn was our first stop after Trefor. It's by far the most remote and self-contained village on the north Llŷn coast. Hemmed in by sheer mountainsides, it's accessible only by a steep winding road with hairpin bends, that takes you perilously close to a three hundred foot precipice and certain, spectacular death. The village has had more comebacks than Tom Jones. Over the years it's thrived, and then subsequently died, as a fishing village, a farming community and as a centre for quarrying, before making its boldest renaissance a couple of decades ago as the national centre for the teaching of Welsh. A historian noted a couple of centuries back that the people of Nant Gwrtheyrn were "the most ungodly on the whole of Llŷn, who spent their whole time feasting and drinking." Definitely my kind of place.

And with that kind of reputation, no surprise to find a politician lurking there. Paul Flynn, the defiantly non-New Labour MP for Newport West, was staying overnight, and expressed his admiration for the place and the visionaries who worked so hard to bring it into being and transform the derelict village. Nant Gwrtheyrn was, he said, a fine example of the old Welsh proverb, *mae'n hawdd cynnau tân ar hen aelwyd*, it's easy to light a fire in an old hearth. This was, as he put it, a place where "people laughed in Welsh, made love in Welsh, had their sorrows in Welsh, and the language seemed to have soaked into the walls". Having seen the S4C reality TV series *Cariad@iaith*, where Welsh learners are cooped up in Nant Gwrtheyrn and filmed twenty-four hours a day in the process, laughing, making love and having plenty of sorrows still seems to be very much part of the place.

Paul Flynn was a great person to interview, largely because he's so good at it. All too often, with people not used to the camera, they'd be chatty, informative and hugely entertaining off camera, but as soon as it was switched on and pointed in their direction, they'd turn into Trappists. No such problem with an MP. He gave good quote, and plenty of it. But then you'd expect that from a maverick politician who got a severe slap on the wrist for daring to suggest that it might help the Welsh economy if the country's legendary magic mushrooms were legalised, for they are, he said with admirable poetry, "the truffles of Wales".

From Nant Gwrtheyrn, we continued along the coast in Ifan's boat, with Geraint Jones still on board. From that vantage point, the old quarries dug out of the mountains in huge steps looked foreboding and very strange, especially in the flat, grey light. In good weather, this rugged coast would be unbeatable. Before long, we were skimming along the huge sweep of beach near Nefyn, under the appropriately watchful eye of the mountain, Y Gwylwyr. Nefyn is northern Llŷn's only town, and was chosen by Edward I to hold a great tournament celebrating the downfall of Prince Llywelyn and the invasion of Wales in 1284. They say that revenge is a dish best served cold. And 700 years should make it cold enough, for, as Geraint recalled "it was here in the seventies that the first holiday home was burnt down by Meibion Glyndŵr. This is where it all started. Happy days," he said with a broad grin. I'm pleased to say that, when that was broadcast, someone with far too much time on their hands and far too much paranoia addling their brain did bother to ring HTV and complain.

As a Sais in Wales, it never ceases to amaze me how rabidly anti their own culture some Welsh people can be. If you live in any one of the struggling communities of rural Wales, it's as plain as the nose on your face just how much damage rarely-occupied holiday homes do to the place. And it's not just the physical lack of people using the resources of the area. It's far more insidious than that. Many holiday home owners bring with them an attitude that could, at best, be described as gently patronising and, at worst, as outright hostile. There comes a point when a critical mass of holiday property is reached and a village dies as a living entity. While not advocating arson, I can truly understand the level of frustration, and, in the face of utter indifference from our elected leaders, the resultant desire to do something powerful and dramatic about it. The Meibion Glyndŵr attacks became absolutely legendary, spawning the famous *Not the Nine O'Clock News* joke "Come Home to a Real Fire. Buy a Cottage in Wales". No amount of polite letter-writing and hand-wringing would have achieved anything like a fraction of that sort of attention to the issue.

As we were travelling around the coast of Wales, it was also becoming increasingly obvious to me that there was a direct link between how Welsh, in language and culture, a coast is and how unspoilt it remains. Coastal areas are amongst the first to be colonised and turned over wholesale to the nefarious demands of tourism, an industry that, if not well-handled, is as subtle as a brick in the face and the respectable economic equivalent of prostitution. The Welsh coasts that remain the most beautiful, wild and unspoilt are also, by no coincidence whatsoever, the ones that have managed, against all the odds, to hang on to their Cymraeg and sense of community. Having sailed around virtually all of the Welsh coast in these two series, I'd say unequivocally that the most inspiring sections are Ceredigion, the Llŷn and Anglesey. You get the picture.

Along the whole of this glorious granite coast, there's only really one major tourist magnet. Porth Dinllaen, now owned lock, stock and beer barrel by the National Trust, is the sweetest honeypot in Llŷn. Protected from the excesses of stormy sea by deep headlands, it's always tranquil there, even more so because there aren't any cars. Here you can relax, take in the views over the mountains of Yr Eifl, mess about on the fishing-boat bobbing sea or stroll the picture postcard beach, all before supping a pint at the Tŷ Coch Inn, just a pork scratching's throw from the sands. It's lovely. But it ain't real any more. It's another Portmeirion fantasy village.

While on land, it gave me a chance to explore some local places, starting at Porthor (sometimes Porthoer), known in English as the Whistling Sands. This is one perfect beach; a westward-looking semi-circle of pale sand backed by tufted cliffs. Its English nickname comes from a phenomenon unique to here, namely that the particles of sand on this beach are exactly the right size to create a kind of squeaking sound as you walk along them. And it really works. A few years ago, I camped the night on the beach with my dog. Every time the mutt disappeared out of the tent, I could keep close tabs on her by just listening to the eek-eek-eek noises as she galloped happily up and down the sand. Neither of us got a lot of sleep that night.

We also filmed a section that sadly never made it in to the final programme. For one very enjoyable, sunny afternoon, I accompanied Lindy Woods, proprietor of the famous Lobster Pot restaurant at Porth Swtan on Anglesey, on her weekly lobster run around Llŷn. She drives her van around the winding, fuschia-flooded lanes of the peninsula, buying a few fresh lobsters here and there from an astonishing network of small fishermen and women. If they have any catch for her, they let her know by putting a lobster pot outside the gate and she'll stop by. Their catch is weighed, she swaps a bit of gossip, money changes hands and then it's off again to the next place. Her whole round takes hours, largely because she's such a popular figure locally and everyone wants to have a chat. One elderly couple, who lived in a tiny bungalow tucked down a remote lane, save her a Sunday lunch every week (her round takes place every Monday, so the gravy hasn't congealed *too* much). They were delightfully unfazed to suddenly find Lindy arrive with a TV crew in tow, and went out of their way to swamp us with tea, cake and biscuits. Their English was patchy, to say the least, and my *dosbarth* Cymraeg couldn't cope with the Llŷn dialect, but it made not a jot of difference to their automatic, and unassuming, hospitality. Many of Lindy's suppliers only have a few lobsters for her, but the money they make on even those is, I could see, an important part of their income. It was wonderful to see such a human-scaled, traditional type of economy still thriving here.

Another greatly enjoyable encounter came with the ebullient priest of Llanbedrog, near Pwllheli, Andrew Jones, who guided me down to the famous Ffynnon Fair, or St Mary's Well, right at the tip of Llŷn on Mynydd Mawr. From here, you gain the classic image of Bardsey Island, its rounded mountain and long tail of land giving it the unearthly appearance of a basking whale. Above the well, tough Llŷn sheep graze in the ruins of an old chapel that would once have ministered to the pilgrims catching their boat to the island from here. I'd been here a couple of years earlier, and spent a fruitless hour or two trying to find the well. Thankfully, with Andrew to guide me, this time I finally got to see it, and it was well worth the wait (no pun intended). Rough steps, hewn straight from the rock in the early medieval period, guide you precariously down to a rocky cleft in the cliffs. The well, which is flooded over twice daily at high tide, reappears like magic, still full of fresh, clear water. It was a hot day when we were there and I plunged my face in the pool and drank greedily. The water tasted like pure nectar. This would have been the pilgrims' last chance for refreshment before the precarious journey across Bardsey Sound to their final resting place.

As well as ministering to his parishioners, Andrew also runs modern day pilgrimages to Ynys Enlli. He's noticed, as he put it, "a huge interest. I've been here for eight years, and I've noticed that, every year, there's an increase in interest in pilgrimage. There's a deep, deep spiritual yearning in people, and to actually participate in a pilgrimage goes a long way to ease that yearning and fill the gap." Amen to that.

The final trip in Ifan's boat, from Porth Dinllaen down to Ynys Enlli and Aberdaron, came on the very last morning of filming for the first series. We'd had an end-of-filming boozy dinner at Helen Williams-Ellis' place nearby the night before, and we were all consequently a bit half-baked the following morning. Conditions were looking a little dodgy, but we were all eager to get it over and done with. I'm ashamed to say that our checking the day's sea conditions got no further than director Emyr looking up a resort forecast on his mobile. The nearest place on the list was Rhyl, and when he announced that Rhyl was due to have a fair day, no-one had the wit to point out the bleeding obvious that that meant precisely bugger all with regard to the sea conditions at the tip of the Llŷn peninsula. It doesn't get much more casually amateurish than that. After an hour or so on the boat, by which time it was tipping down with rain, it suddenly struck me that there was absolutely nobody else on the sea that day. Not a soul. What did they know that we didn't?

Skipper Ifan didn't seem to care either way. He's a Llŷn farmer to his core, with all of the stoic, shoulder-shrugging attitude that you would expect of someone so rooted in the elements of this wild western shore. I was, to be honest, having huge difficulties understanding him, in Welsh or English, as he never spoke without a fag clenched between his lips, and every sentence came punctuated with a demonic, shrieking laugh. In his little plastic tub of a boat bouncing around on the swell, skippered by someone who laughed like a super-annuated Basil Brush at everything, I was beginning to feel distinctly nervous. This was the final journey of the final programme that we'd filmed for the first series. I'd managed to get all this way without yet honking over the side of a boat. Would my luck hold? Or, more to the point, would my stomach?

After Porth Dinllaen, the landscape of the northern Llŷn coast undergoes a radical change. Gone are the bitten-out mountains, sheer cliffs and quarries, to be replaced by a gentle patchwork of farms spilling down to the water's edge. Not that I could see much of it, mind you, as rocky outcrops meant that we couldn't go too near the coastline, much of which was hidden anyway by a veil of that special Welsh rain that gusts sideways in dramatic curtains of water, rather than doing the more obvious rain-like thing of falling vertically down.

And then we started to hit the swell that announced our approach to Bardsey Sound. Not for nothing is Bardsey known in Welsh as Ynys Enlli, the island of the currents, for they are its single biggest defining feature. The funnel of water between the island and the mainland has one of the worst reputations anywhere on these islands. Add the worsening conditions to the fact that we were pushing against the tide, and you see how things started to go seriously pear-shaped.

To give you the clearest indication of just how rough conditions can get here, consider the tale of the couple recently arrived on Bardsey as new wardens. Two or three years ago, they left the island at Christmas to get some provisions from the mainland. They had to wait forty-eight days until conditions had calmed down sufficiently to allow them to return home. Forty-eight days to get back from Tesco's. Now that deserves some serious Reward points.

I was just making the point in a piece to camera that Bardsey Island is known as the "island of twenty thousand saints", when we hit some spectacularly high waves. Just as the words "and it's the island where

Sailing to Ynys Enlli in happier, calmer times (pic Lou Hart)

people went to die" came out of my mouth, the boat pitched drunkenly and a wall of water smacked us all. "And I'm really beginning to know how they felt!", I hollered, just as the camera tipped over and chaos broke out. People started shouting, doors slammed open and shut, there was water everywhere and I hung on like grim death, something that seemed quite possibly imminent.

Isn't it amazing how well we can kid ourselves sometimes? While the camera was trained on me, I was doing my utmost not to show the increasing panic and feeling of nausea that was rising in me. As soon as the camera was switched off (or, in this case, once it had crashed over), I squealed like a six year old girl, but at least I thought I had kept my cool while being filmed. Not a bit of it. When, a couple of months later, I saw the footage for the first time, I realised how tragically deluded I'd been in this belief. I looked terrified. I was bloody terrified. If you want proof, look at the stills on the front cover.

And it got worse. A lot worse. We couldn't actually land where we'd intended to at Aberdaron, because the waves even there were too high and rough to get us to the beach in Ifan's little ship-to-shore rowing boat. My heart sank into my boots when it was announced that we'd have to go back out to sea and continue round the coast, hopefully to land at

Abersoch instead. Conditions were, by now, atrocious and that last ten miles or so took forever. We'd completely abandoned the filming by now, concentrating instead on staying alive, if at all possible. Ten, twelve foot waves crashed all around us, sending everything scattering. Even Ifan had stopped his hyena cackle. At one point, the rowing boat we were towing snapped free of its mooring and disappeared into the angry, churning swell. The radio didn't work, Ifan had no distress flares, and I was seriously beginning to wish that I'd told those people close to me that I loved them. Fortunately, the brief appearance of a mobile phone signal on Emyr's phone enabled him to ring ashore. Double fortunately, there was a second cameraman, David, on land, filming us from there. He's a local lad and a member of the sailing club at Abersoch. He promised to get a boat out to meet and rescue us.

Suffice to say, David was true to his word. Once we'd rounded the bottom of Llŷn and entered Cardigan Bay, the swell dropped considerably, but the relief of getting off that boat was one of the most intoxicating feelings I'd ever had. And I finally threw up, for the first – and, as it proved, the only – time. Not on the sea, but within a minute of putting my feet down on solid earth, the tension and terror finally got the better of me and I gracefully vomited into the hedge at the side of the Abersoch Sailing Club car park. Sorry, fellas.

Our journey, however, was supposed to have finished in Aberdaron, many miles and many stomach somersaults earlier. It's a wonderfully atmospheric village, the final stop for many an Ynys Enlli pilgrim before they crossed to the island. Unlike Abersoch, which has become a kind of outpost of Cheshire for the yachting and surfing sets, Aberdaron is sombre and spartan, but always breathtakingly beautiful. Just like the poetry of R.S. Thomas, the finest English language poet of the twentieth century, whose last ministry was here in the capacious parish church at the head of the beach. Thomas, who came within a hair's breadth of winning the Nobel Prize for Literature, wrote with savage illumination on matters of faith, belief and nature, but he hit the mark most thrillingly when, as in this poem *The Small Window* he wrote about the land he loved with all his heart and soul.

> In Wales, there are jewels
> To gather, but with the eye
> Only. A hill lights up
> Suddenly; a field trembles
> With colour and goes out
> In its turn; in one day

You can witness the extent
Of the spectrum and grow rich

With looking. Have a care;
This wealth is for the few
And chosen. Those who crowd
A small window dirty it
With their breathing, though sublime
And inexhaustible the view.

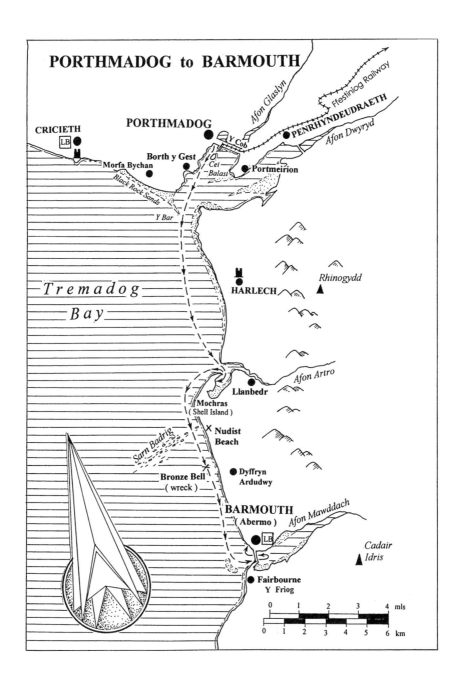

PORTHMADOG to BARMOUTH

CRICIETH
LB

Afon Glaslyn

Ffestiniog Railway

PORTHMADOG
Y Cob

PENRHYNDEUDRAETH
Afon Dwyryd

Borth y Gest
Morfa Bychan
Cei Balast
Portmeirion

Black Rock Sands

Y Bar

T r e m a d o g

B a y

HARLECH

Rhinogydd

Afon Artro

Llanbedr

Mochras
(Shell Island)

Sarn Badrig

Nudist
Beach

Bronze Bell
(wreck)

Dyffryn
Ardudwy

BARMOUTH
(Abermo)
Afon Mawddach
LB

Cadair
Idris

Fairbourne
Y Friog

| 0 | 1 | 2 | 3 | 4 | mls |
| 0 | 1 | 2 | 3 | 4 | 5 | 6 | km |

58

CHAPTER FIVE:
PORTHMADOG - BARMOUTH
Beached Wales

Porthmadog? After Aberdaron? Well, yes. As there wasn't enough coast left in Wales to warrant a third series of *Coast to Coast*, squeezing as much as possible into two series meant that some places didn't get looked at, and the southern side of Llŷn was one of them.

It would, I know, have been a lot of fun. Abersoch is well-geared up for a good time, Llanbedrog is a gorgeous village and beach, Pwllheli has its eerie West End and button-bright marina and Criccieth – well, just think of that view as you sweep along the main road from Porthmadog and suddenly crest the hill to see the castle and the bay spread out before you. It gets my heart racing every time, and I'm sure from the sea, the castle and town would have looked quite majestic.

In the programme that we filmed from Porthmadog, we did go to Black Rock Sands at Morfa Bychan, although the sequence never made it into the final edit. I was, er, lucky enough to be given a ride on the back of a jetski by the Gwynedd County Council Beach Warden. It's his job to keep the many other jetskiers and powerboat owners in check, usually by turning up his throttle to the max and outmanoeuvring them in the aquatic version of a handbrake turn. Black Rock Sands, out of season an absolute peach of a beach, is, in the height of summer, a rather depressing monument to the cult of the Boy Racer. After paying your couple of quid, you can drive right on to the sands – indeed, the beach is, officially, the largest public car park in Gwynedd – and, if no-one's looking, have a quick go at being one of those land speed record heroes by hurtling along the flat sand. For many people, the sort who get an attack of the paranoid heebeejeebees if they move out of sight of their car, it is the ideal mixture of car park and beach, and it never ceases to amaze me to see dozens of people picnicking happily around their Vauxhall Astras. As one of the designated jetski and motorboat beaches in the area, it also attracts that speed-loving crowd. At least it keeps them all in one place, and leaves the other spectacular Gwynedd beaches to the rest of us.

This boat journey was all about beaches, as we were travelling down the longest – and many would say finest – in Wales. It's a curious stretch, for although this is the old county of Meirionydd, one of the Welshest in the north-western *bro Gymraeg*, the coastal strip, that few miles between the Rhinog mountains and the sea, has been heavily anglicized for decades and rings to the sound of Midlands accents.

Not our first port of call, however. Porthmadog is firmly Welsh and feels a great deal older than it actually is. It came into being only in the early nineteenth century, when entrepreneur and Lincolnshire MP William Madocks decided to drain and dam a great swathe of the Glaslyn estuary, re-route the river and reclaim the land as pasture. To that end, he built the mile-long embankment known as the Cob, that brings both road and rail into town. In recent years, the road – the main A487 – has been widened, hallelujah! No longer do you have to face death by oncoming bus.

The railway that also crosses the Cob is the Ffestiniog narrow gauge line, the single biggest draw to Porthmadog for tourists. I have to say that I am deeply sceptical about Welsh tourism's over-reliance on steam trains and their often pointlessly tiny stretches of track. But it's hard to be too churlish about the Ffestiniog Railway, whose thirteen mile journey, snaking up the mountains to Blaenau Ffestiniog, is one of the undisputed wonders of Wales. It also makes Porthmadog a kind of Alton Towers for trainspotters, many of whom can be found studying the videos and books in the station shop with the same sort of rapt, panting concentration that you only ever otherwise see amongst punters browsing in a sex shop. I rest my case.

Porthmadog's a lively wee place, and it always has been. It was the traffic in slate and shipbuilding that once kept the harbour stratospherically busy, as schooners laden with the world's best slate departed for all points north, south, east and west. On returning from their long voyages, the very last thing the boats would do before docking would be to jettison tons of rubble taken on board as ballast to steady the ship on its homeward journey. Over the years, this ballast grew into a small artificial island, known as Cei Balast, which is accessible only at low tide.

And so it was that the crew and I squelched our way through the mud to Cei Balast one gloriously sunny Sunday morning. It's a haunting spot. Unbeknownst to locals, the ballast that was dumped here carried with it the seeds and spores of foreign plants. Botanists have traced the mysterious spread of exotic flora back to this little bump of Wales and many strange wonders still grow here; the most celebrated of which was named the Welsh Bladderwort.

Strange flowers, and some pretty wacky rocks too. I'm absolutely no geologist, but even to my amateur eye, the variety of rocks and stones on Cei Balast is astonishing. Within a minute or two, I'd found, nestling cheek-by-jowl, a stonking great lump of flint, a smooth chunk of chalk, a silky piece of marble, some pure quartz, some glittering granite and a lump of anthracite. They could have come from anywhere, but they have all landed in the beautiful Glaslyn estuary under the mountains of Snowdonia.

So on a perfect, glassy Porthmadog morning, I started my journey down the coast to Barmouth. It's a two-legged affair, courtesy of the Gwynedd Beach Patrol. Porthmadog Harbourmaster Dafydd Phillips took me to the southern limit of his patch – just seven miles down the coast – to Mochras, more commonly known as Shell Island. We glided out of the estuary, past the smart villas of Borth-y-Gest, easily the most des res address round these parts, but, as ever, mostly comprised of holiday homes.

With Dafydd Phillips, Porthmadog harbourmaster

Before long, we were out in the Bay proper and Dafydd could crank up the speed of his powerful motorboat. "We're out of the six knot zone now," he said with undisguised glee as he pushed the boat into instantaneous acceleration. I felt as if my stomach had stayed still while the rest of me surged forward. It's strange, because we only hit a maximum speed of 25 knots (about 30mph). When you're doing that in a car, it feels as is you're practically walking. In a boat, it feels immeasurably faster. Indeed, a speedboat is by far the quickest way of seeing this stretch, as you can avoid the huge estuaries that punctuate the coast and force road traffic into all kinds of tortuous twists and turns.

Not only was this a journey along fine beaches, our route also connected two of the most luscious estuaries on the Welsh coastline, from the Glaslyn down to the Mawddach. The Glaslyn shares its estuary with that of Afon Dwyryd, nestled against whose shore is one of the most iconic sights in all of Wales, indeed all of Britain: the fantasy huddle of Portmeirion. Usually described – rather lazily, I think – as an "Italianate village", it always feels firmly Welsh to me. That blend of beauty with eccentricity, community with colour is Wales at its very best. And the fact that Clough Williams-Ellis searched the world for the perfect site for his grand folly, and then found it just six miles down the road from his family home, is a tidy metaphor for the Welsh condition... Look what's on your own doorstep! There are riches beyond measure.

Seeing Portmeirion on its headland, framed perfectly by the woods, the bay and the mountains, is phenomenal. But it also makes me feel faintly sad, because this wonderful, evocative memorial to the human urge for useful beauty, finished only twenty or so years ago, reminds us that, within just a few decades, we've drifted even further away from the principles that built this place. Can you imagine, for one tiny minute, Clough's original proposals for Portmeirion landing on the desks of a modern council Planning Committee? They'd laugh it out of the chamber in seconds flat. "A 'home for fallen buildings'? On a sensitive piece of coastline? You must be mad! Now, let's get back to the business of building out-of-town megastores and Legoland housing estates." Portmeirion reminds us that each age has its architectural legacy, and, apart from a few showpiece buildings, ours is looking pretty grim.

Back at sea, we're really motoring, and the great sweep of Harlech beach passed by in a blur. The overwhelming feature of the town from the sea, just as it is from the land, is the castle, easily the most solidly satisfying of all the Edward I fortresses of northern Wales. It's the position that makes it so splendid, and it would have been even more impressive when it was first built and the sea lapped at the foot of the great rock on which it was built. This was a fortress designed to intimidate, and, my god, it still does. Its other major feature is its relative intactness. It takes little imagination to visualise pennants fluttering from the turrets and men in chainmail parading the battlements.

It's only a few minutes further and we're motoring gently through the complicated channels of the Afon Artro estuary into the harbour at Mochras, or Shell Island, now one huge campsite. This was very exciting for me, as I've been coming to the island for years, but never by boat. Normally, I'd have to chance my luck on the causeway that gets cut off at high tide. Only once have I been caught by the tide, although the wardens of Shell Island have a thousand stories of towing embarrassed punters out of the rising waters or rescuing people whose engines have been rendered useless by the salt.

For over half a century, Shell Island has been a refuge for people who want their holidays to be as free and unfussy as possible. So many modern campsites are awash with rules and run by people who'd be more at home running an army camp. No running, no showers after 9, no dogs, no noise, no fires – no fun. Blimey. So much for the old free and easy camping holiday.

But you can get just that at Shell Island. It's still head and shoulders above the rest. There are lots of special ingredients to the place. For starters, it's on a sublime piece of coast. It's also huge, apparently the largest tent site in Europe. And – one of my favourites, this – caravans are not allowed. You keep them out, and you also keep out caravanners – the sort of people whose idea of fun is to hitch up a mini-replica of their suburban semi to the back of their car, and then drag it around the country at a steady 40mph. Good riddance.

Shell Island is also a bit of an invisible tribal border. This is where the holiday areas of northern Wales, the traditional ground for folk from Merseyside, and central Wales, where most of the punters come from the West Midlands, meet. And still most of the accents you'll hear at Shell Island will either be Brummie or Scouse. It's a funny old mix, but it does seem to work, especially when it's lubricated with a few pints down the island's pub. Lord only knows how many lads from Dudley have gone home with a new bird (or bloke) from Birkenhead, and all thanks to the magic of Mochras.

The beach that heads south from Mochras yawns eight miles to Barmouth in a glorious unbroken sweep of sand and glittering sea. One remote part of the beach has, for about seventy years or so, been a favourite of naturists, or nudists. For decades, their presence was just about tolerated, and then five years ago, after a lot of argument and argy-bargy, Gwynedd County Council took the step of declaring a section of the beach officially nudist, to date still the only official such beach in Wales. Mind you, barely any one of these trips went by without the skipper, at one point or other, pointing out an unofficial nudist beach on the patch we were visiting. I am pleased to report that the entirely to-be-

Just to prove that I really did go for it on the nudist beach.

encouraged activity of letting it all hang out on a beautiful Welsh beach is alive in all corners of the country.

To reinforce the official sanctioning that nudity has here, and only here, they've whacked up signs all over the place warning the casual passer-by that – eek! Shock horror! – you might encounter people with their kit off. One side of the line, you keep your clothes on. The other, Gwynedd Council say you can strip off without a care in the world. And, boy, is it worth doing. If you've never swum naked, you just don't know what you've been missing.

Like a herd of migrating wildebeest, the nudists of Dyffryn Ardudwy

As nudity tends to get such a naff nudge-nudge, wink-wink treatment on telly, I was mustard keen to do a celebratory piece in the programme about the Dyffryn Ardudwy nudist beach, but the obvious question was how to do it. Whichever way I thought around it, there was really only one obvious thing to do – whatever I said, I had to get my kit off. The idea was that I delivered a piece to camera and then walked away towards the sea, stripping off as I went, in a shameless parody of the title sequence in *The Fall and Rise of Reginald Perrin*. I would then plunge eagerly into the waves. This was one of those bits of filming that really needed to be done in one take, and I'm relieved to say that we all got our jobs right first time and it was duly done.

Before wetting my bits'n'bobs in the surf, I'd noticed a (fully-clothed) couple watching our activity with a fierce level of scrutiny. Once in, I swam around for a while, before emerging, dripping wet and very happy. The couple marched over towards me.

"What are you filming?" the woman snapped.

It was a question we got all the time, so I rattled out my off-pat answer: "It's a six part series for HTV about the Welsh coastline." She didn't look impressed.

"Do you have permission to be filming here? Don't you think it's rather intrusive?"

"No, we haven't filmed anyone so that they could be recognised, we can't. And yes, we do have permission to be here from Gwynedd County Council, since you ask."

"Prove it," she shot back. "Where's your permission? Show it me."

Let me just backtrack here a little. Here was a woman, wrapped in a fleece and trousers, demanding ID from me, who was somewhat disadvantaged by virtue of being stark bollock naked. "Well, where the bloody hell do you think I might have hidden it? If you want to conduct a full cavity search, help yourself" was what I wanted to say, but I managed to bite my lip, and instead sent her off to harrass Emyr the director while I got dressed, muttering darkly under my breath. I really couldn't have said a civil word to the daft bat, but Emyr, bless him, was mollifying and diplomatic to a fault. His later theory was that, as they couldn't possibly have been objecting on the grounds that they might get filmed naked, they must be a couple away on an illicit dirty weekend, a fact unknown to their respective partners back home, and were paranoid about being caught out on the TV. It's a plausible theory. Or they could just have been bad-tempered pillocks with voyeuristic tendencies.

For the second leg of my coastal journey south from Shell Island, I joined Barmouth Harbourmaster Keith Allday aboard his county council speedboat. Keith's worked on boats all his life, and is obviously completely dippy about the sea, because in his spare time he's the coxswain of the Barmouth lifeboat.

From the sea, the most immediate impression of this tranche of coast is its stupendous setting. The Rhinog Mountains hem in the coastal flatland, and it struck me how much life and commerce in this area must have been utterly dictated by the harsh terrain. Only really in the twentieth century would road travel in this area have arrived. Prior to that, the only ways in or out would have been by sea or on one of the drovers' routes that wind their way up through the passes in the mountains. This area of land, known as Ardudwy, was well-documented as the roughest, and poorest, in Wales, and transport difficulties were integral to that. Ardudwy is also home to many of the finest prehistoric remains in the country, many bearing names to do with Ireland, suggesting that the main early colonisation of this area came from across the water, rather than via the M54 as it is these days.

Not that the sea route was an easy one either. Lurking just below the water is Sarn Badrig, St Patrick's Causeway, an underwater reef over ten miles long that looms large in legend as one of the remaining features of the Cantre'r Gwaelod, the Lowland Hundreds (for more on which, see the next chapter). To avoid running aground on Sarn Badrig, we had to hug the shoreline and keep an eye on the landmarks that told us when we're near. Keith points out that, where the two main Rhinog mountains meet and form a V, the causeway starts just here. You can, he says, walk on Sarn Badrig on very low spring tides. Although we couldn't see it that day, so calm were the conditions, you can often get a great view of the causeway, and how it divides the sea into different coloured patches, from the nearby mountains.

Over the centuries, Sarn Badrig has been responsible for the loss of countless lives in Cardigan Bay. It wasn't even charted on maps until the mid eighteenth century. Hundreds of ships, blown off course by south-westerly storms, were wrecked within sight of these beaches. They lay undisturbed until the advent of scuba gear allowed divers to uncover their secrets. We hooked up with one of the local diving enthusiasts, Tony Isles, who struck it lucky soon after starting to dive, happening upon the remains of a three hundred year old, 700-ton Genoese galleon. Since its original discovery, the Bronze Bell wreck – as it's come to be known – has yielded some amazing treasures.

Before we started filming, Tony said that he didn't want to give too many details away on camera as to what the Bronze Bell wreck had produced or precisely where it was. Fair enough. But then as soon as the camera was switched on, he seemed to forget his own restrictions, and enthusiastically told us just about every detail of the treasures found and all but gave the grid reference of exactly where we were. You can hardly blame him – it is an amazing story. Exquisite carved silverware and thirty cannons were found, but the most exciting piece of the cargo was a few dozen stone blocks, that the divers originally thought were probably concrete. They transpired to be blocks of Italian Carrara marble, the very finest marble ever quarried. None has been produced for over a century, and suddenly, here was tons of the stuff lying on the bed of a Welsh bay. So what was it doing there and where was it heading?

Tony has a very plausible theory on this one. In the late seventeenth century, St Paul's Cathedral in London was being redesigned and rebuilt by Sir Christopher Wren after the Great Fire of London in 1666. The accounts of the rebuilding show that an order was placed with an Italian marble works, and a later note in the margin states that the order never arrived. Was this the marble intended for St Paul's?

Due to the massive raft of restrictions that govern finds from shipwrecks, only two blocks of the marble have been allowed to be shifted and raised to the surface. One was used to date and identify the find, the other was given to the nearby town of Barmouth, where a public competition was held to see what the townspeople wanted to see done with it. The rest of the blocks, it seems, will have to spend eternity slowly crumbling to dust in Cardigan Bay.

So back on the boat, and after miles of sandy beach, the trappings of the seaside industry became ever more numerous as we neared our journey's end. First the caravan parks loomed into view, and then the houses and hotels that announced our imminent arrival in Abermo, Barmouth. And we were definitely a lot closer to those hills. The coastal strip narrows to almost nothing here, meaning that Barmouth has had to squeeze itself into any available spot. Houses cling to the cliffs, are built practically on top of each other and face in all different directions in a gloriously haphazard riot of slate and stone. Amazingly, centrestage in all the barely contained chaos is the enormous Victorian parish church of St John, its haughty gaze out to sea seeming to set it apart from the higgledy-piggledy town around it.

As a special treat, Keith took me on a detour under the magnificent Mawddach estuary bridge. I'm a complete sucker for bridges, and this is one of the best. One hundred and thirteen rickety wooden spans escort the Cambrian Coast railway 2253 feet across the mouth of the most sublime estuary in Wales. Don't just take my word for it. The Mawddach has been heartily eulogised by dozens of writers and artists, ever since Wordsworth and Coleridge trotted over the mountains to drool at the view.

One of the first things we saw after docking at Barmouth was the sculpture that had been carved from the piece of Carrara marble found in the wreck of the Bronze Bell just down the coast. Entitled *The Last Haul*, it was carved by local sculptor Frank Cocksey and he lives, I was told, high on the cliff overlooking the town. Numerous alleys dart off the main street and up on to The Rock, as it's known, where dozens of small fishermen's cottages cling precariously to the cliff. There are no cars or roads here, just a dizzying labyrinth of alleyways, steps, arches and sudden gracious little

*The view from
The Rock at
Barmouth*

courtyards. It is breathtakingly beautiful and I can't believe that, in dozens of trips to Barmouth, I never knew that this village-within-a-village even existed. If it were all whitewashed, you'd swear you were exploring some little Spanish fishing hamlet.

Frank does indeed live right at the top of The Rock, just below the summit which has the distinction of being the first piece of land in Britain to be acquired by the National Trust, way back at their very beginning in 1895. He's lived here, high above Barmouth, for over 40 years, working in forestry and on the sea, but his abiding passion has always been sculpting. Since retiring he's been free to pursue his art full time. Working in his al fresco studio, he enjoys a truly enviable view over the Mawddach and the ocean. He's spent countless hours up here carving his sculptures from wood and stone, but little did he dream that one day he'd be working the most highly prized marble of the Italian Rennaisance.

"In my crazier moments," he said, "I think it was destined. Someone put it on a ship in Genoa, they shipped it all the way down here, it was shipwrecked and then it sat there waiting for three hundred years for somebody to come along and do something with it, and that was me."

Frank took me down to the quayside to show me *The Last Haul*. Seldom have I seen a piece of public art that inspires such affection in the public – every time I've been near it, there's always a few people nearby gazing in rapt admiration. It portrays three generations of fishermen all pulling together one huge catch out of the sea. The bottom half of the block, however, has not been touched. Three centuries of underwater corrosion has left the surface fabulously pockmarked, and you can still see the odd shell of a mollusc or two hidden in the holes. The marked contrast with the silky smooth carved part of the marble only makes it even more impressive.

The inspiration for the sculpture came one day as Frank was down by the water one night with his sketchbook. Three fishermen, a grandfather, father and son, were struggling in howling wind and squally rain to drag in a netful of fish. As they came ashore, battered and exhausted by the experience, the older man turned to Frank and said "that's it. That's my last haul. I've had enough." He wasn't the only one, and now the monument commemorates not just the local fishing industry, but its demise, for it has all but disappeared on any real commercial level.

Like so many towns on the coast, Barmouth's sole remaining industry is tourism. To that end, it's unashamedly populist and attracts most of its holidaymakers from the Midlands. This has given the town a rather schizophrenic air. You've got the slate built fishing village around the harbour and the souvenir shops, amusements and fairground rides alongside the beach. Gibraltar and Blackpool all in one. Plus a large dollop of dear old Brum. On the way into Barmouth is a well-known local landmark, the Birmingham Garage, hunkering down in the least Brummie-like situation under the sheer cliffs. It always occurs to me when I drive past how hollow a joke the name is. For those who have sat in a sweaty family car for three or four hours, to be reminded of the place they've just left must be a right treat. And I'm sure local folk love being reminded of just how few of them are left in their own home patch. Less awkwardly, there's another Brum export in Barmouth, and it's where we finished the journey. Baltis – that Kashmiri spicy stew that's served in the dish in which it's cooked and properly eaten with a nan bread, rather than cutlery – are Birmingham's finest gift to the world. Cultural evolution is to thank for the Welsh take on the Balti – I ate a wonderful lamb and freshly-caught salmon Balti, and it was exquisite. As was the whole journey. I felt stuffed with good food, sunned and salted by the elements and stirred by the fragile beauty of all that I'd seen. Life's a beach.

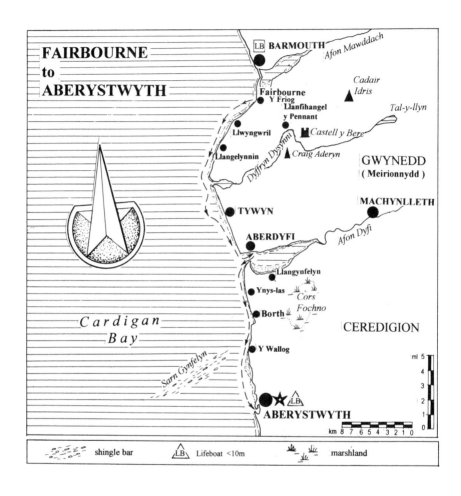

FAIRBOURNE
to
ABERYSTWYTH

LB BARMOUTH
Afon Mawddach

Fairbourne
Y Friog
Llanfihangel
y Pennant

*Cadair
Idris*

Tal-y-llyn

Llwyngwril

Castell y Bere

Llangelynnin

Dyffryn Dysynni

Craig Aderyn

GWYNEDD
(Meirionnydd)

MACHYNLLETH

TYWYN

ABERDYFI

Afon Dyfi

Llangynfelyn

Ynys-las

*Cors
Fochno*

Borth

*Cardigan
Bay*

CEREDIGION

Y Wallog

Sarn Gynfelyn

ABERYSTWYTH

ml 5
4
3
2
1
0

km 8 7 6 5 4 3 2 1 0

shingle bar   LB Lifeboat <10m   marshland

70

CHAPTER SIX:
FAIRBOURNE - ABERYSTWYTH
Home is where the Heart is

This journey was possibly the one that I was looking forward to the most, as it offered me the chance to take a look at a very familiar coastline from an altogether new angle. I've lived in this area for the past four years, and have spent countless hours on the beaches and cliffs of this beautiful central tranche of Cardigan Bay. But, as ever, eager to diss what I don't like as readily as to praise what I do, I wanted to kick off our voyage in Fairbourne, across the other side of the Mawddach estuary from Barmouth. It's a little town that most definitely falls into the first category.

There's a definite whiff of colonial decay about Fairbourne, a place that was built solely as the plaything of a wealthy English industrialist and which never seems to have integrated itself into Gwynedd or the real world. And in a land so depressingly dependent on tourist steam trains, Fairbourne takes this strange obsession to its logical conclusion in the shape of the toytown, tiny-gauged Fairbourne Railway, which shuttles passengers two miles from the mainline railway to the Barmouth ferry. En route, it passes what used to be called the Golf Club Halt, but which was recently renamed in a bid to outdo Llanfairpwllgwyngyllgogerychwyrndrobwllllandysiliogogogoch and bring moribund Fairbourne the same kudos, and coachloads of tourists, as its Anglesey rival. The halt is now known as Gorsafawddacha'idraigodanheddogleddollônpenhrynareurdraethceredigion, or the "station on the Mawddach with dragon's teeth on the north Penrhyn Drive on the golden Cardigan Bay sands". If only to show how tortuously overblown the name is, the "dragon's teeth" are a set of grim concrete defences left over from World War II. And that's about as good as Fairbourne gets.

Three years ago, I wrote a piece in *Planet* magazine about English incomers into Wales, and their often patronising and even racist attitudes. As an incomer myself, with traces of a Midlands accent, I know that I've been told things that these people would never dream of saying to locals. The level of ignorance of and hostility to Welsh culture, most especially towards *yr iaith Gymraeg*, is horrifying, and seems often to be worst from people who admit that they've moved here to escape black and Asian people in the big English cities. They don't see the irony of becoming the immigrants themselves here that they so detest back home, nor, like their perceptions of the people they complain about back in Wolverhampton or Stockport, do they do anything to integrate themselves in the local culture or community. In the article, I used the example of Nick Griffin, UK leader of the avowedly racist British National Party, who moved to the Dyffryn Banwy in Montgomeryshire, and acknowledged in a *Guardian* interview that he'd done so specifically "to avoid multi-cultural Britain". He's not been the only one.

The article came out during the febrile summer of 2001, when barely a week went by without some Welsh v English dust-up being spread over the front pages. Whether it was Anne Robinson's ill-advised sneers on *Room 101* or apocalyptic warnings from Welsh luminaries about the effects of English migration into the country, this ancient grumble rolled on and on and on. My piece became the headlines for a day or two, even making it to the front page of a few of the London broadsheets. As a result, a reporter from BBC Radio 4's flagship *Today* programme contacted me as he was interested in doing a report about the phenomenon. We met in a cafe in Borth, and he was very sceptical. "Are there really great numbers of anti-black, anti-Welsh people moving to Wales?", he asked. I assured him that, in my experience, there were. "So where do I find them, then?" he demanded. This was a toughie – after all, who is going to be prepared to have a microphone stuck under the nose while they fess up to being a racist lowlife on national radio? And then I thought, hmmm, try Fairbourne. He did. I met up with him two days later at the end of his fact-finding mission and he was gobsmacked. "The place was just crawling with people prepared to slag off black and Asian people *and* the Welsh. What are they doing here if they hate it so much? I couldn't believe it."

So, it was no hardship to get out of the place aboard Mike Harris' fishing boat, *Ma Chipe* (it's Breton, apparently). To give Fairbourne some credit, at least it's in a spectacular location, and from the sea it looked even better. With the proud ridge of Cadair Idris standing sentinel over the sublime Mawddach estuary, all basking in the shimmering heat of a baking hot summer's day, the view was delicious.

The scenery quickly changed as we headed southwards. Craggy cliffs, topped with impossibly green fields, faced us now. Cut out of the almost sheer slopes are both the main A493 and the Cambrian Coast railway, phenomenal pieces of engineering in such difficult terrain. On the map, there appears to be a railway tunnel just here, although when you see it, it's more of a two hundred yard long roof that's been built over the line. This is where a landslide took place in the early twentieth century, burying the track and almost closing the railway for good. The roof was subsequently built to ensure that any falling debris misses the track and the trains.

Past Llwyngwril and then we caught sight of the tiny, scattered hamlet of Llangelynnin. This is rural Meirionydd at its most appealing, the shoreside church the ancient centre for this parish of upland farmsteads. Each farm name, complete with the name of the family who owned it (and, it's to be hoped, still do), is inscribed on the rustic old box pews inside the church, a feature that was once common in Wales. As Llangelynnin was, fortunately, too remote to be done over by the restorative zeal of the Victorians, the box pews have survived, and are now grade one listed.

A mile south, the coast road turns sharply inland to avoid the surging peak of Foel Llanfendigaid. There's a great campsite just here, right above the half-sand, half-shingle beach that's never busy, even on the hottest day. The beach is backed for the first section by cliffs, and gaping large out of one of them is Ogof Owain, reputedly the cave where Owain Glyndwr hid out during his rebellion of the early fifteenth century.

By now, we were all sweating like the proverbial glassblower's armpit. The temperature had climbed into the nineties, and even a cooling sea breeze was having little effect. I was itching to leap into the sea – after all, how can you do a series about the Welsh coast without sampling the goods, as it were? Mike kindly dropped anchor, and the crew filmed me leaping in. I didn't have to fake my rapture; it was gorgeous, and not at all cold, even though we were at least a quarter of a mile out from the shore. Dave the cameraman, Helen the director and Guto the researcher all followed me in to the water and for a few happy minutes, life was just perfect as we all splashed around like ten year olds. Helen had packed a particularly delicious picnic hamper, which we then sat around on the upper deck demolishing. I think we all had one of those "blimey, I'm being paid for this" moments.

There was a lot that I wanted to get into this programme, so, more than ever, we had to make some tough choices as to what to include and what to leave out. Even with comparatively short bursts of the Welsh coast, there are so many stories to be told, histories to be uncovered, places to explore and people to talk to. Not everywhere can be featured. And so it was that Tywyn got dismissed in pretty much one sentence as it flashed past. My feelings for Tywyn are pretty similar to my feelings for Fairbourne, although, to be fair, there's a great deal more history and colour to Tywyn. This is, after all, the place where the earliest example of written Welsh, dating from around 650AD, can be seen on the magnificent St Cadfan's Stone in the town's impressive parish chruch. Right at the other end of the taste spectrum, Tywyn also became a brief legend in the 1980s when a local vicar was imprisoned for cutting the penises (or is that penii?) off corpses in his care, before pickling them for his very bizarre, and deeply scary, private collection. Just thinking about it makes your eyes water.

I did, however, want to include a valley – the Dyffryn Dysynni – near Tywyn that was once an inland sea fjord. Land that used to be sea is as much a feature of this coast as the more famous "lost" Cantre'r Gwaelod, sea that used to be land.

I'm often asked where's my favourite place in Wales. My answer is usually "well, it depends on what mood I'm in", as different landscapes surely suit different frames of mind or moods. It's one of the things that makes me delirious with joy, that, within half an hour of my front door, I can be in the sea, on a mountain or moor, in a forest, by a waterfall, in a river meadow or stomping my way down a huge beach. But there is one place that probably comes as close as any to being an outright winner for my affections, and that's the Dyffryn Dysynni. Everyone that I've ever taken there has been absolutely overwhelmed by its charged atmosphere and raw beauty, just as I was the first time I encountered it a decade or so ago.

The valley courses inland from near Tywyn, and shudders to a halt below the back side of Cadair Idris, twelve or so miles inland. Up at the Cadair end are the hugely atmospheric ruins of a native Welsh castle. Castell y Bere feels like a place that has witnessed, as well as the inevitable battles and sieges, a hell of a lot of good times too. Built by Llywelyn Fawr in 1221, it was the grand palace of Gwynedd in its day, rising imperceptibly from its rock as a beacon of hospitality and heartiness to its guests. It feels part of the landscape, not imposed upon it, as in the great invaders' castles at Caernarfon or Pembroke. And it was here in this valley, after a picnic in the ruins on a beautiful spring day four years ago that I finally decided to upsticks across the border to Wales, settling just a few miles up the road. Of all the big decisions I've ever made with my life – haircuts, lovers, jobs, cars and so on – that was the one that has never, ever caused a shred doubt or regret. This is home.

A short hop down the lane from Castell y Bere brings you to the charming little church of St Michael at Llanfihangel-y-Pennant. Its setting is enough to make anyone want to pick up a paintbrush, but it's for another reason that I return here time and again, and that's to see the magical 3D map housed in the vestry. It's a map of the valley constructed in patchwork and cloth, fourteen feet long and to a scale of one foot to one mile. Twenty or so local volunteers built it, each walking a patch of the area, getting to know every field and fence, stile and stable, before reconstructing their corner in material. Every time I see it, I find the map utterly inspirational, combining as it does such a reverential sense of place with such a beautiful, creative way of expressing it.

The map has an exaggerated vertical scale, so that the contours are higher than in real life. Even without that, Craig Aderyn (Bird Rock), that prehistoric-looking knobble in the middle of the valley, would still stand out, as it does from both the sea and looking back from Castell y Bere. Jane Whittle, a local artist who was largely responsible for getting the map project up and running, joined me, and my dog Patsy, for a walk up Craig Aderyn. Considering the fact that we had blazing hot sunshine for almost all of the week of filming, sod's law dictated that as soon as we climbed to get some upland views, a sea mist blew in and blanked out everything. We went for it all the same, and it was a hoot. Helen, the director, Emyr, the cameraman and Dafydd, the sound man, would position themselves somewhere on the climb and Jane, Pats and I would amble past them through the mist, chatting as we went.

Eight thousand years ago, at the end of the last Ice Age, the sea retreated from this valley, but no-one's ever told the cormorants who nest on Craig Aderyn. Every day, they fly out to sea, collect fish, and return towards dusk to their inland sea cliff. With views completely blanked out, we had to rely on our other senses to confirm their presence. The odd telling squawk and the definite tang of fish and sea salt in the air was all we had to go on.

Back on *Ma Chipe*, we ventured along the gorgeous strand of beach that goes all the way from Tywyn to the corner of the Dyfi estuary at Aberdyfi. It's all backed by sand dunes (not surprisingly, as that is what the name Tywyn means) and the Aberdyfi golf course, apparently one of the best in Wales. Aberdyfi is very popular with golfers and boatie types and has rapidly become one of the property hotspots of the area, mainly for holiday homes. Ann Clwyd, the fiery Labour MP for Cynon Valley, has a retreat here, as does Tory ex-Chancellor Kenneth Clarke, which must make for an interesting alliance over a pint at the Penhelig Arms. I'm sure that they, and the other well-heeled visitors, are enthusiastic punters of the town's newish status as something of a gourmet haunt.

Aberdyfi looked great as we threaded our way through the bars and sandbanks that sit in the mouth of the Dyfi estuary. The town has been supremely blessed by its position, facing south over the Dyfi and the sea with a sheer backdrop of soft green mountains. Straggled along the shore, with houses of different hue placed at all angles and contours, and a massive Victorian chapel pride of place in the middle, you look at it and you could only possibly be in Wales. I was lucky enough to live over the other side of the estuary for a year and a half, and the view over Aberdyfi was mine from the living room window. Since moving inland, I particularly miss the heart-stopping sunsets, as the windows of the town blazed with pink fire and the hills mellowed under a rosy glow.

There are, of course, a few people hereabouts who resolutely manage to ignore any signs of Welshness, even here in Gwynedd. There's an acid test, and that's how they spell the name of the town, Aberdyfi or Aberdovey. Both options still appear on most road signs in the area, which seems to be blanket bilingualism at its craziest. Aberdovey is just an anglicized corruption of the name, one that's only been in use for a comparatively short period, and, as such, could easily be despatched into the history books. Fair enough if a town's English and Welsh names are very different – Caergybi/Holyhead for instance – but if the English name is just a lazy re-spelling of the real Welsh name, why not just stick with the original? I can well recall my fascination with Welsh road signs when I was first getting to know the country as a nipper in the 1970s. More often than not back then, any sign would be daubed with paint and slogans, which I loved and thought to be very exciting. It's great that the campaign bore fruit and that all signs are now in both languages, but there surely must be a case to be made to dispense with some of the superfluous English words? This point always comes to mind when I'm driving along the M4 and see the turn-off signposted for

Parc
Margam
Park

– is there really anyone who wouldn't be able to work out quite what

'Parc' meant?

As we left Aberdyfi's lovely old wooden quay, numerous lads, having spotted that we were filming, hurled themselves off it for the benefit of the camera, and hit the water with varying degrees of theatricality. It happened a lot on these journeys, especially during the filming for the second series in the glorious summer of 2003, and it always brought a grin to my face. Open up any newspaper or turn on the TV and you'd believe that kids these days are all three stone overweight and spending most of their time on the playstation or being stalked by perverts in internet chat rooms. Countless times during the filming of *Coast to Coast*, we saw evidence to the contrary: kids mucking around, hanging out with their mates, having a laugh, being adventurous, enjoying the great outdoors – just as they always have, and always will.

On the other side of the Dyfi estuary from Aberdyfi is the dune system and beach of Ynyslas. When I lived up the road in Llangynfelyn, this was, nine times out of ten, the venue for my daily walk with the dog. Here, I've swam in the sea at daybreak on May Day (very cold indeed), watched a lunar eclipse in January, built and lit fires, thrown thousands of sticks for Patsy, constructed a stone-and-shell memorial to a friend who'd died, sunbathed, swam, boogie boarded, danced and cwtched. Even now, although Aberdyfi or Tywyn beaches are technically closer to where I now live, I'll nearly always go to Ynyslas or Borth for my fix of seaside light and air.

Borth is – and this is meant with no disrespect – far more downmarket than Aberdyfi, and, for that reason alone, I love it. I pray that the place won't become as gentrified as so many other coastal communities have in recent years. Long may the place keep its gritty heart and its cheerfully quirky atmosphere. For those who don't know it, Borth is, basically, one long straight street running for a mile and a half along the beach. It is, I've read, the only town built in Britain on a storm beach. Its vulnerability marks it out – there's none of the steadfast, staunch backing of the mountains, as at Aberdyfi or Aberystwyth, here. Borth is strung out, two lines of houses, between a vast beach and a vast peat bog. The most telling view of the town, where its fragility is most apparent, is from the main A487 near Tal-y-bont. Looking out over the miles of the Cors Fochno bog, dissolving into an endless western sea, Borth appears between the two like a rickety set of rotten teeth that could be punched out by the weakest of throws.

It is, perhaps, that sense of living on the edge that gives the place its unique oomph and atmosphere. When we were planning the second series, my idea for getting a take on Borth was to accompany the local postman on what surely must be one of the most difficult rounds in Wales. No house in Borth has a number, instead virtually all of the properties have an address which is simply Name of House, High Street, Borth, Ceredigion. Houses are tucked away behind each other, annexes have grown into fully-fledged properties, names are sometimes changed, and through all that, the postie has to cope.

Borth's regular Royal Mail rep is the delightful Mary Gittins, and doing the round with her one grey morning was a real highlight of the series. Her round – the long, straight stretch of Borth – covers nearly five hundred properties, and her knowledge and understanding of the community she serves with such unfailing good humour is wonderful. Everyone gets a chat if they want one, she darts in and out of kitchens leaving the morning's mail on the table and her spare arm is permanently occupied in the serious business of waving as she shuttles her way up and down the long street. One old lady, a real Borth *grande dame,* came to the door wrapped in a kimono and smelling faintly of gin. She chatted to Mary for over ten minutes, and, to be honest, made little sense. Afterwards, I asked Mary why she made such an effort. "I'm probably the only person she'll see all day, you know," she replied. "It's really important to have even just a little human contact."

People even seemed amazingly unfazed to open their door to Mary and find a film crew staring back at them. No surprise, given Borth's high proportion of artists, performers and all-round creative types, that a fair few people played up to us as if we were talent scouting. You can tell that this is a place where self-declared intellectuals like to congregate just by visiting the gents' toilet in *The Friendship Inn,* a real gem of a pub hunkered down on the landward side of the High Street. The wall above the urinals has been handed over to the punters as a place for freeform graffiti; you can even borrow a marker pen from behind the bar. Much of the stuff is painfully self-conscious and probably sounded a great deal better after four pints. The one that nearly had me peeing over my shoes in amused amazement is an appendix to someone else's graffito, correcting their punctuation. "GRATUITOUS APOSTROPHE" reads the addition, with a handy arrow pointing out the offending mark. It made me yearn for a few illiterate "CCFC"s and "For a good time, ring....", the standard graffiti of a public gents'.

Borth, if legend is to be believed, is the last remaining town of the Cantre'r Gwaelod, the Lowland Hundreds. Every country has its legends of lost lands, and of course Wales – a nation that can spin a good yarn out of thin air – is no exception. The most celebrated Welsh Atlantis is the

Cantre'r Gwaelod, the flat, fertile land that lay under what is now Cardigan Bay. Legend has it that this was a paradise on earth, home to sixteen golden cities, with the sea being kept at bay through an elaborate complex of sluices and gates. Unfortunately, the gatekeeper got hideously drunk one night and fell asleep on the job. His few shandies too many cost the lives of hundreds as the sea roared in and took the land.

The ancient fossilised forest on Borth beach (pic MP)

Even if the legend is a load of old baloney, it undoubtedly harks back to folk memories of when the sea was indeed much further out. But instead of sixteen wealthy cities, chances are the land was covered by forest, and between Borth and Ynyslas, you can actually see some of the ancient tree stumps, emerging out of the tide twice a day as they have for millennia. A couple of years ago, I was there and found some oak leaves emerging from the sand around the stumps. At first, I didn't really think anything of it, but then it suddenly hit me that there are absolutely no living trees anywhere near. The leaves – shiny and pliable like leather – were definitely coming from the sand, and so must surely have hailed from this crop of trees. I've still got a few at home, and the thought that they are probably at least five thousand years old is, somehow, deeply humbling.

An even more potent reminder of the Cantre'r Gwaelod comes in the five sarnau, or causeways, that stick out like ghostly fingers into Cardigan Bay. Although scientists like to say that they are but moraines left by retreating glaciers, it's far more appealing to think of them as ancient roads or even walls of the lost land. We'd already had to skirt around Sarn y Bwch near Tywyn, and I'd heard plenty about Sarn Badrig near Barmouth in the first series. But my favourite is Sarn Cynfelyn at Wallog, a couple of miles south of Borth. At low tide, the reef of stones unfurls itself into the ocean for hundreds of yards. It's perfectly possible to walk along it (slippery rocks notwithstanding), and experience the very strange sensation of waves gently crashing either side of you, fuelling all kinds of power-crazed fantasies of walking on water or parting the waves.

An ancient route? Sarn Cynfelyn near Clarach (pic MP)

Dave (Dai) Williams came to join us off Borth in the Aberdyfi lifeboat, a superb piece of equipment that was paid for by money raised in the West Midlands borough of Sandwell – one of many, many examples, both good and not-so-good, of the mutual relationship between the Midlands of England and *y Canolbarth* of Wales. Dave is a warden with the Snowdonia National Park, as well as being a lifeboat volunteer. It's impossible to overstate how important these volunteers are in small seaside communities. I'd felt queasy enough on a few of our sea journeys on calm summer days, and I was getting paid for it. To take out the lifeboat to an SOS call on a raging winter's night takes courage and commitment beyond my comprehension. Not only do they perform jobs

Brits at play: Llandudno seafront (pic M.P.)

Three for the price of one: the bridges of Conwy (pic M.P.)

Telford's triumphant bridge over the Menai Straits (pic M.P.)

The dramatic coast of Holy Island (pic M.P.)

Perfect peace: sunset over the Barclodiad-y-Gawres burial chamber (pic M.P.)

Llanw 1 and Llanw 2 (pic Dewi Glyn Jones)

Looking down the coast of Pen Llŷn (pic M.P.)

Mynydd Carnguwch on Llŷn, more popularly known as Carn Tit (pic M.P.)

Llŷn peninsula from near Porthmadog (pic M.P.)

Instant relaxation: the view from Shell Island towards Harlech and Eryri (pic M.P.)

*How to squeeze a film crew into a toy train: Dafydd, Helen and Emyr
on the Fairbourne Railway (pic M.P.)*

Checking my facts before opening my mouth – for once (pic Helen Williams-Ellis)

The mist descends: Patsy and I ready to climb Craig Aderyn (pic Helen W-E)

Chilling out in a Ceredigion sunset (pic M.P.)

Vulnerable Borth and secure Aberdyfi from the Ceredigion Coast Path (pic M.P.)

Dedication to duty: Emyr – still bandaged from his accident in Pembrokeshire - being winched up in the Bosun's Chair (pic M.P.)

Druidston Haven beach, one of Pembrokeshire's finest (pic M.P.)

Mike, Emyr (complete with fresh leg wound)
and Dafydd Parry aboard the Predator (pic Guto Williams)

Turquoise sea and purple rocks – it could only be Pembrokeshire (pic M.P.)

that few of us would dream of attempting, they also have to spend considerable time recruiting and training new blood. As Dave explained to me, in a place like Aberdyfi, there is massive competition for volunteers, as the mountain rescue team, the lifeboat, the coastguard and the fire service all depend on them, and, in effect, are all chasing the same few people. And with the exodus of young people to the big cities and beyond, it's a perpetual struggle.

I asked Dave about the Cantre'r Gwaelod and what his thoughts about it were. One of the features of the legend are the famous bells of Aberdyfi, clanging mysteriously out to sea as a mournful reminder of the lost cities. Dave told me that, when a storm has just passed, and the air is still but the sea still churning, his imagination often does indeed hear something that sounds like church bells far out at sea.

The last leg of the journey was something of a repeat of the first part, with cliffs, farms and a wild sense of remoteness swiftly overtaking the mood, and so different in flavour from the wide expanses either side of the Dyfi estuary. Despite the similarities, I was aware that we'd crossed quite a boundary, not just from Meirionydd (or Gwynedd) to Ceredigion, but from northern to southern Wales. The Dyfi provides the border, as it has for at least one and a half thousand years. So deeply ingrained is the north-south split in the Welsh psyche, that it really does feel as if some chasm has been spanned as you cross the first road bridge over the river, some fifteen miles inland near Machynlleth. If a sentry box and red-and-white mechanised barrier appeared on the bridge tomorrow, it wouldn't look out of place. Even at sea, there was an imperceptible shift, a hint of something more mellow and softer in the air, as we continued south along the Ceredigion seaboard.

Whichever way you arrive in Aberystwyth, it will be impressive. On land or sea, the town is surrounded on all sides by miles and miles of gaping emptiness, giving it the appearance of the Emerald City at the end of a very long rainbow. And from the sea, it looked wonderful: stately, self-assured and as deeply rooted as an old oak, sandwiched so perfectly between its two sentinel rocks of Constitution Hill and Pen Dinas. For me, Aberystwyth is the real capital of Wales. Unlike modern upstart Cardiff, which looks defensively over the muddy waters of the Bristol Channel towards southern England, Aber's gaze, from its position at the very heart of Wales, is expansive and endless, limited only by the sunset on the distant western horizon. This is a town whose nationalism is firmly of the internationalist variety. Here, the Welsh and English languages jostle along easily enough together, augmented by a Babel of other tongues, tantalising snatches of which are heard along the Prom.

It's also a place for fun. With a well-earned reputation for convivial living, Aberystwyth is where Welshness – still a bit starchy and self-conscious elsewhere – relaxes with its toes in the surf and a pint in its hand. And where drink forms the vanguard, sex will surely hotfoot it behind. Aberystwyth, its sea breezes fanning the famously lusty Welsh flames, is a strangely sexy town. Not in that nudge-nudge, naughty postcard way so beloved of English seaside resorts, but a dirty, honest horniness that gets all the suggestive small talk out of the way and just goes for it double quick. No surprise that, when Christianity overcame the Celtic bishopric of Llanbadarn Fawr, Aberystwyth's precursor a mile or so inland, the one change refused by the locals was that priests should be celibate. God and no sex? A contradiction in terms! The carnal theme continues, six hundred years later, when parish lad Dafydd ap Gwilym wrote a metrically precise poem inspired by the view in church of the *Merched Llanbadarn*, the women of Llanbadarn:

Plygu rhag llid yr ydwyf,	Passion doubles me over,
Pla ar holl ferched y plwyf!	Plague take all the parish girls!
Am na chefais, drais drawsgoed,	Because, frustrated trysting,
Onaddun'yr un erioed.	I've had not a single one.
Na morwyn fwyn ofynaig,	No lovely, longed-for virgin,
Na merch fach, na gwrach, na gwraig.	Not a wench nor witch nor wife.

A further six hundred years on, and even a bored bard would have little trouble getting laid in this salty, spicy town. The air – on a summer's night, there's an almost Mediterranean tang in the fuschia-flooded alleys and back lanes – hangs heavy and sweet, and Aber's lust expresses itself across the boundaries. Welsh, English, Catalan, Creole, resident, visitor, straight, gay, serious, dabbler, who's counting? Surfers, high on adrenaline from the Cardigan Bay waves, pound the beat around the seafront bars, a heady, libidinous mix of dazzling sunsets, thumping techno lite and cut-price beer. Regular pulses of incomers – students, academics, conference delegates, day-trippers, holidaymakers and those up town from the yawning rural hinterland of mid-Wales – keep faces fresh and options open. Even up against urbane Cardiff or racy Swansea, this resort of just 14,000 souls has been rightly named (much to the alarm of *The Western Mail*) as the "gay capital of Wales". Metropolitan queer activists, waving their placards at bishops and ministers, might sneer, but Aberystwyth is the only place where the Queen, in all her half-century reign, has had to cut short a visit due to a protest. Centre stage on the demo, six years ago, was a local drag queen anointing and knighting her mock subjects in stack wig and stilettos.

While not all Aberystwyth's politicking turns out so camp and colourful, its beliefs do veer towards a good-natured anarchic radicalism. Again, this is in total contrast to any comparably sized English resort, where curtain-twitching, cardy-buttoned Conservatism rules with an iron grip. Even when Aber pulls its socks up and smooths its hair down, no-one is really convinced. In 1905, at the height of Edwardian pomp and circumstance, the announcement was made that the town had beaten Cardiff as the site for the National Library. A celebratory torchlight procession through the streets was planned, fast degenerating into hapless farce. Hardly any of the Town Council showed up, none of the lifeboat crew and the few students who made it were noted to be "a half disorderly crowd of gownless and capless boys". The ceremonial band argued amongst itself as to where they should be on the procession, the debate becoming so heated that the big drum player stomped off in a huff, leaving his ragtag ensemble without their marching beat. To make up the missing numbers, a rotary round brush jalopy and three municipal watering carts took up the rear. It was, as the *Cambrian News* wearily noted at the time, "the poorest procession Aberystwyth has ever seen".

For all these reasons, and many more, Aberystwyth is my kind of town, and it was a delight to arrive there in such style as the sun was

Capital of the Canolbarth: Aberystwyth (pic MP)

sinking low towards the horizon. From the clapped-out colonialism of Fairbourne to the inspirational internationalism of Aberystwyth; this really had been a journey from the ridiculous to the sublime.

After filming in Borth and Aberystwyth the one morning, I had a very different kind of afternoon in the town's magistrates' court on the prom. I was called to give evidence against a bloke who had gatecrashed my birthday party the previous December and, when asked to leave as he was causing offence to a fair few of my guests, proceeded to lose the plot completely, smashing the front windows and door of my house with slate wall blocks, before whacking a mate of mine with an iron bar and cracking two of his ribs. This had all happened just a couple of days before Christmas, and had, unsuprisingly, somewhat overshadowed my festive season, not helped by the fact that it took my insurance company three bloody months to the day to sort me out a new front door. The whole experience had been awful, and I wasn't looking forward to the court case at all. But filming this programme during the week of the trial helped enormously, because it reminded me of what a fantastic part of Wales I live in, and how many wonderful, kind, interesting people there are in the area.

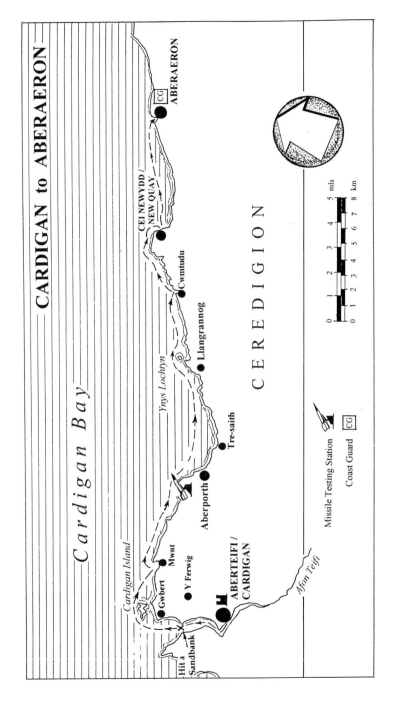

CARDIGAN to ABERAERON

Cardigan Bay

Cardigan Bay

ABERAERON

CG
ABERAERON

CEI NEWYDD /
NEW QUAY

Cwmtudu

Llangrannog

Ynys Lochtyn

Tre-saith

Aberporth

Cardigan Island

Mwnt

Gwbert

Y Ferwig

ABERTEIFI /
CARDIGAN

Hit a
Sandbank

Afon Teifi

C E R E D I G I O N

Missile Testing Station

Coast Guard   CG

								5 mls
0	1	2	3	4				
0	1	2	3	4	5	6	7	8 km

85

CHAPTER SEVEN:

CARDIGAN - ABERAERON
far from the Madding Crowd

It's a pretty standard convention in television that the strongest episode should be the first in a series like *Coast to Coast*. This journey was always the frontrunner for that accolade, and it was the first broadcast in the first series in February 2003. The reasons for the episode's strength were, quite simply, a magnificent boat and an equally magnificent coastline, both probably the best we ever encountered in either series.

First, the boat. *The Keewaydin* (the name apparently comes from *Hiawatha*) is an irresistible early twentieth century wooded sailing ketch, eighty foot in length and with two main masts from which canvas sails billow in the breeze. Rescued by owner, and our skipper, Paul Welch from certain mouldy death in Malta, he bought the boat for a princely £1 and spent painstaking years restoring her to glory. And glorious she is. At every stop on the journey, we drew crowds of eager onlookers, snapping away with their cameras and yelling questions about her to us.

The journey will always stand out in my mind, for I think that this section of Ceredigion is the best of the entire Welsh coastline. It absolutely blew me away. Towering cliffs, idyllic beaches, rolling farmland and one of my favourite Welsh seaside towns – New Quay – all combined with the splendours of the *Keewaydin* to make for a very happy trip.

Without any doubt, Ceredigion is one of the finest counties in Wales. It's big, it's beautiful and its people, the Cardis, might well suffer a bit of a reputation for the tightness of their wallets, but there's no tightness when it comes to their enthusiasm and kindness. And yet Ceredigion is still relatively unknown – especially when you compare the areas that sit either side of it. It's propped neatly between two very well-known National Parks, Snowdonia to the north and the Pembrokeshire Coast to the south. In many ways, it's got loads of the fine features of both, some of the mountains of Snowdonia and the awesome coastal scenery of Pembrokeshire, but receives just a fraction of the attention or the visitors. All the more for those of us that love the place, I'm glad to say.

Rather neatly, our journey took us from the old county town, Aberteifi or Cardigan, to the new one, Aberaeron, although neither are the county's main metropolis, if you could possibly call Aberystwyth such a thing. Cardigan is a very pleasant kind of place, but it does rather remind me of the item of clothing of the same name: it's comfy and easy enough, but it's not exactly a byword for elegance or style.

Now I found this very hard to believe, but folk locally claim that Cardigan once ranked up there with London and Liverpool as a trading port. Over 300 ships were registered here in its heyday. The port's decline was hastened by the arrival of the railway and the silting up of the river Teifi. The river's never been dredged, so that today navigating your way down to the sea is a bit like treading an invisible tightrope, especially when you're in a great hulk like the *Keewaydin*. The day we sailed was one of the few tides high enough to get us out of the estuary, but it was still on a bit of a wing and a prayer, as we chugged down the river along the boundary between Pembrokeshire, on our left, and Ceredigion on our right. The sun was out, the scenery was splendid and all was looking perfect. Then, just as the open sea loomed almost close enough to touch, a bump ricocheted around the boat and we ground to a sticky halt. We'd hit a sandbank.

It's times like this when I realise what a useless git I am. I have no practical skills at all, and in the flurry of activity that then ensued, all I could do was to hover around in the background, making what I hoped were vaguely helpful noises of encouragement. Richard and Myles, two of Paul's crew, were despatched to go and jump up and down on the very end of the main boom. I can't quite explain the physics of such a manoeuvre, but, hey, it did the trick and we were soon seabound once again.

In the nineteenth century, Cardigan was the main Welsh port for transatlantic passenger crossings, most for emigration purposes to the New World. What would they have been thinking at this point in their journey? Huge excitement, great sadness, anticipation and raw terror must have been ingredients in the potent cocktail coursing through their veins as they looked back at the very gentle view I was now enjoying, of

Gwbert-on-Sea and the mouth of the Teifi estuary. This would have been the emigrants' last ever sight of their homeland. Did they try and stare so hard at it that it would imprint on their souls, so that they would never forget a single detail? Some, I'm sure, would have been. Others would have been on the ship's bow, head held high and straining to see into the future ahead of them.

We cruised around Cardigan Island, now a nature reserve, before meeting the coast proper. Immediately, a perfect cone of a hill dominated the view, a few miles away at Mwnt. I'd never previously understood how Mwnt – the Mount – came by its name. On land, the hill that shelters the tiny whitewashed church and generous cove hardly seems to merit such a grand title. But from sea, it's a wholly different story. The Mwnt is a fine, proud peak that soars to a pinnacle before plunging straight down into the sea. It would have been an automatic marker point on any sea journey up Cardigan Bay.

A slice of the Greek islands in Mwnt (pic MP)

We moored in Mwnt Bay and took the rib to shore. It was, to be honest, one hell of a shock. After a few miles of swirling seabird cliffs and velvet green opulence, accompanied by no more noise than the gentle splash of the waves, suddenly to find ourselves on a packed beach on a summer Sunday was terrifying. It was like Piccadilly Circus with added windbreaks. Mwnt is a perennially popular beach. It's west-facing, sheltered, sandy and, most important of all, it has a large car park and somewhere flogging Cornettos. Just before doing this journey, I'd read a survey that said that about 80% of people, when on holiday or days out, never travel further than *a quarter of a mile* from their car. Isn't that incredible? You could have gone a few miles up the coast, and, if you were prepared to walk for fifteen minutes or so, have found a beach that you'd have virtually to yourself.

Even with the crowds, Mwnt is a beguiling spot. It's much-photographed little white church, sat all alone on the cliff tops like something from a Greek island, is supposedly the oldest in Ceredigion, and it certainly feels deeply settled and sacred. Even before a church was erected on the site, there was a huge pilgrim's cross on top of the Mwnt, which must have made for both a cheering and chilling sight as pilgrims and traders battled their way up and down Cardigan Bay.

I was aching to get back to the boat, however, and soon we waved the crowds a relieved goodbye. Our pilgrimage continued north, past the missile testing station at Aberporth. Not only do British forces test their missiles out to sea here, but any old dictator in the world can (and does) hire the facility, making Cardigan Bay the biggest missile testing range in all of Europe. It's not a slogan that the local tourist board have adopted.

Having been pleasantly surprised by the lack of development so far, Aberporth delivered something of a double whammy, with both the missile station and in its position as the beginning of Caravan Park Ceredigion. This is the southern limit of the traditional holiday area for West Midlanders, and, hailing from that area as I do, I know all too well just how crucial to your holiday is a sea view, so rarely do Midlanders get to see the ocean. The caravans, lined in rigid rows with their biggest windows staring blankly out to sea, always remind me of battalions of tanks poised for hostile action, and they looked even more like that from the sea.

A few minutes later, we were passing the altogether prettier beach at Tresaith. It has the two essential ingredients of fine sands and a great pub, but the *pièce de resistance* is when you come out of the sea all wet and salty after a swim, there's a waterfall spilling right onto the beach where you can shower off. I always fondly remember Tresaith as the first place that my dog, Patsy, encountered the sea. To a rescue dog scooped up off the streets of inner-city Birmingham, this strange, churning, relentless wall of water bore no resemblance to the oily canals and park ponds that she was used to. She climbed up a rock and stood there, every sinew straining, as she barked and barked at the waves. Occasionally, she'd venture down to sniff at the water's edge, but then a wave would come in and she'd leap theatrically out of its way, managing to look simultaneously surprised and thoroughly indignant. She ended up drawing quite a crowd, and I was sorely tempted to pass the hat round.

It wasn't quite such an impressive performance the first time she actually got to swim in the sea. Pats is a born swimmer, but it was on the gentler shore at Shell Island that she first plucked up the courage to dip her paws in properly. Unfortunately, she gets hyper-excited when swimming, and ends up drinking loads of the seawater. For those who haven't had the good fortune of experiencing a dog in this situation, let me just say that seawater acts as a very concentrated combined laxative and enema to a dog. I'd got her out of the sea, and we were walking along the huge expanse of the beach, when she suddenly sneezed. That momentary spasm relaxed all her muscles for a split second, allowing a great jet of brown water to shoot out of her rear end, like one of the Kuwaiti oil wells that needed capping at the end of the Gulf War. Pats stared in surprised amazement at her bottom, while I – caring owner that I am – was laughing so hard that I'd collapsed onto my hands and knees in the sand. A passing family hurriedly moved their fascinated children on.

The section of coast between Gwbert and New Quay is infinitely easier to negotiate on sea than on land. The only roads connecting the hamlets and villages hereabouts are narrow, tree-lined, winding little lanes that quickly disorient you and cause endless rows between drivers and navigators. After Tresaith, it was therefore a real surprise how quickly we reach the very pretty, and very popular, old fishing village of Llangrannog, wedged tight into its little river valley. House prices here are sky high, way beyond what most locals can afford. Consequently, most of the village houses are holiday homes, making any sense of community almost impossible to maintain. It's the same story all over, but it makes it no less infuriating each and every time it's encountered.

Mention Llangrannog to many of my Welsh mates and they will go into misty-eyed reverie about snogging someone very unsuitable after a bottle of Strongbow at the village's Urdd camp when they were fifteen. There's a wonderfully *Hi-de-Hi* atmosphere at the camp, which has been giving Welsh-speaking kids a blast of seaside air since the 1930s. Mind you, they've had to update a bit, and these days you can even try *bwrdd eira*, snowboarding, on their artificial ski slope.

The next section of coast, past the promontory of Ynys Lochtyn and the iron age hillfort at Pendinas Lochtyn, was the grandest spectacle of all on this most magnificent of journeys. Sheer cliffs rose out of the sea, peaking at over seven hundred feet, the highest in Ceredigion. Waterfalls tumbled down the rockface, birds swirled and swooped and we were all left open-jawed at the ball-breaking scale of the scenery. A sharp and sudden break in the cliffs came at the tiny, rocky little cove of Cwmtudu.

This wild, impenetrable stretch of coast has always been an ideal location for smugglers, and Cwmtudu, ideally placed in its remoteness to avoid the long arm of the law, was always the top spot for landing illegal booty. Local poet and historian Jon Meirion Jones met up with me to tell me more about the area. I was particularly fascinated by his tales of the Teulu Cilie, the family of nearby Cilie farm, who have been legendary in eisteddfodic circles for well over a century. This whole area is a bastion of traditional Welsh literature, and I would hazard a guess that there must be more eisteddfod chairs lurking in farmhouses round here than in any other part of Wales.

Jon gave a characteristically eloquent explanation of why this was. "Well, the terrain adds to the romance, of course," he explained. "The area was self-sufficient in its economy, and self-sufficient in its culture too." It is the recognised capital of the *cynghanedd*, that precise metrical lilt, full of alliteration and internal rhyme, that so characterises bardic Welsh poetry and affords great opportunity for romance, beauty and ribald humour. To illustrate the pattern in English, John told me of an *englyn* – the kind of verse written in *cynghanedd* – written by one of the Cilie boys to a pretty girl who had sent him her photograph.

> *You are fit in your photo, – yes indeed*
> *Nice and tidy also,*
> *Sweet as jam, no sham, no show -*
> *Ready to marry tomorrow?*

Back on the *Keewaydin* in the fading light of dusk, I was feeling poetic and inspired by the swashbuckling smuggling atmosphere of Cwmtudu. Smuggling is yet another thing on a very long list that seems to have dulled with the years. Landing forty thousand fags from a Calais hypermarket just doesn't quite have the same romance as the barrels of rum and gunpowder of yesteryear.

The approach to New Quay, our overnight mooring, was stunning, although there was a noticeable increase in the sheer quantities of bird crap over the cliffs as we got nearer to the town. Creaking round the final corner of cliffs, the reason became all too apparent in the shape of the fish processing plant at the town's edge. I have never seen so many seagulls congregating in one place. The noise and stench was just overwhelming.

Having been feeling like Ioan Gruffudd in *Hornblower* all day, I suddenly started to feel more like Tippi Hedren in *The Birds*. I'd really rather have stuck with Ioan.

We dropped anchor a little way out in New Quay harbour. After a delicious dinner in the galley kitchen, a few of the boys decided to take the rib in to the quay and go to the pub. Remembering the shock of Mwnt beach, I decided to stay put and sit out on deck, watching the town's cheery night-time twinkle across the water. All eight of us – four film crew, four boat crew – were staying on the boat, in tiny little bunks separated only by curtains. I had one of the best night's kip in ages. The boat was rocking gently in the harbour, and the sensation was wonderful, like being rocked to sleep as a tiny child. Even the creaks and belly groans of the wooden boat, and the odd splutter and snore from elsewhere on board, only enhanced the fairy tale quality of the experience.

The next day was our chance to explore New Quay. It's a fabulous little place, a real gem, as well as being something of an optical illusion. From the water, the town looks really neat and orderly, appearing to consist of three straight parallel streets one above the other. Go on land, and it's all a lot more confusing than that. Cobbled streets duck and dive, connected by rickety alleyways and passages that deposit you where you least expected to be.

New Quay is a town of real character, and one of real characters too. I was fortunate enough to hook up with Susan Passmore-Jones, published historian and doyenne of an ancient local family. Guto, the researcher, and I spent a fabulous afternoon at Susan's house while we were recceing this programme. Not only does she know her subject inside out, she also uses the most finely-tuned and illuminating turns of phrase, in English or in Welsh. To listen to her was to bathe in elegant erudition. For the interview, I spoke to Susan overlooking the harbour.

The town, I put to her, has always had a very individualistic streak. "Oh yes it has," she replied. "For so many people here, places like Buenos Aires were a lot more familiar than Birmingham, for instance, and they brought back new ideas. New Quay's always been very outward-looking and independent." She spoke of the days when sailing dominated everything in this tight-knit community, and recounted a tale told to her by one of her schoolteachers. "When my teacher's dad was a boy, he went to the pier on an errand and one of the boatmen said, 'hey, we're short-handed, come aboard.' 'Tell ma I won't be home,' he said to a younger sibling, as he climbed aboard the vessel. He was gone for three years. There wasn't a lot of fuss about it, you just got on with the job."

Susan was off that afternoon to an auntie's ninetieth birthday party.

"New Quay's a wonderful place for nonagenarians, you know," she told me. "Possibly it's the air, and just because it's a happy place. It's always been a rather lotus-eating place to some extent." I loved that. They should put it on the town signs: "Welcome to New Quay – A Rather Lotus-Eating Place". It would sure beat those dreary invocations to visit yet another "Historic Market Town" or "Heritage Port".

One character, no stranger to lotus-eating (as long as someone else bought it for him), who was famously attracted to New Quay was, of course, Dylan Thomas. He and his young family lived here briefly during the latter part of the second world war. For many years, New Quay played down the connection, but as the period recedes further into history and the libellous scars and debts that he left fade, the town has come out and proud with its Thomas connection and now plays it for all it is worth. A recent book, *The Dylan Thomas Trail* by local author David Thomas (no relation) guides the reader around the old drunkard's favourite local haunts. No surprise, then, that many of them are the town's pubs. Of the accounts given by David Thomas in his book, two particular pubs caught my eye. One was the grand Hotel Penwig by the harbour, which, he says, was "during the war, one of the centres of New Quay's active and varied sex life". I say. The other, almost next door, is the down-to-earth Blue Bell, "a favourite of boys from the boats, who hosed themselves down on the flagstoned floor when they needed to sober up." The very first Mr Wet T-shirt contests perhaps?

Dylan's favourite boozer of them all was the Black Lion, and it was there that events started on the fateful night that saw him and his family leave town under a very large cloud. He had been drinking and winding up an army officer, home on sick leave from the war. The officer, convinced that his wife had been engaged in some kind of ongoing threesome with Dylan and Caitlin Thomas (not impossible, it has to be said), went back home at closing time, picked up a machine gun, and then walked to the Thomas' rundown chalet on the edge of town and blasted it with gunfire. It is said that one bullet narrowly missed one of the children. The officer was charged with attempted murder, and the Thomases left New Quay shortly afterwards.

In his book, David Thomas asserts that New Quay is as near a place as any that could claim to be the principal inspiration for Llareggub, that scabrous little town that acts as the setting for *Under Milk Wood*, Dylan Thomas' most enduring work. And he's probably right. That mix of harbour and harlotry, prudery and priapism, bombazine and beer is, even now, the flavour of New Quay, far more so than Laugharne in Carmarthenshire, the Thomas' later home and somewhere that likes to think of itself as the "real" Llareggub.

New Quay has always seemed to be a place that knows how to have a good time. It works hard and plays hard, and I loved it the very first time I saw it, about twenty years ago. A decade later, I got together a group of mates to rent a cottage near the town over the New Year holiday, which I'd heard was celebrated particularly fiercely in New Quay. There were about six of us going down from Birmingham, meeting four other friends coming from London. For some reason, I thought I'd memorised the address of the place, and didn't bother bringing the letting agency's letter with me. Suffice to say, the name I'd memorised wasn't the name of a house, but a whole sweep of rural Ceredigion, and the cottage remained obstinately unfound. My mates weren't impressed, and, from our base camp in a local pub, sent me off knocking on every farm door in the dark and asking if anyone had seen our house?

If some English prat turned up on my doorstep after dark and told me he'd mislaid his holiday cottage, I suspect my first reaction would be a very hollow laugh. But the good people of the New Quay area took me in, gave me tea, something stronger if I fancied it, rang round their friends and made as many enquiries as they humanly could. All to no avail. By now, it was late in the evening and we still had no place to lay our hats and call our home. The pub, now doing a roaring trade out of my very pissed-off friends, said that they could put us up for a tenner each, but there was no breakfast and we'd have to be out by eight as the landlord was off to visit relatives. "Fine!" we shouted as one. I pointed out that I could ring the letting agency in the morning and sort out the problem, so we all settled down for some slightly better-tempered beers. At one point, the landlord asked me what I did for a living, and when I told him I was a travel writer and had just finished the first edition of the *Rough Guide to Wales*, he cracked up on the spot. "Now I've heard it all," he wheezed through his mirth, "a bloody travel writer who's lost his holiday cottage. That's priceless."

Needless to say, by the next morning, we were legendary in the area, and everywhere that we went over the next week, within a forty mile radius, people would say "oh, are *you* the lot who lost your cottage? Duw, duw, we did laugh." Everyone also told us that New Quay was *the* place to go out on New Year's Eve, as loads of people get togged up in fancy dress and parade around the pubs. It sounded great, but as our cottage (we did find it eventually) was a fair few miles outside the town, and none of us had brought our St Trinian's outfits, we decided to go to the nearest pub in a small village (I'm not saying which one) just a mile away, instead.

What we hadn't reckoned on was that we were in the pub to which all those New Quay revellers who'd ended up losing in either a fight or a break-up retreated to lick their wounds, quite literally in some cases. It was the district Sin Bin for the night. Thus it was that, as we sat in a corner trying to be as upbeat as possible, a succession of casualties came crashing through the door, most still in tattered or blooded fancy dress, and looking either like thunder or suicide. My most abiding memory is of one poor bloke, dressed up as a rabbit, who'd obviously had a possibly terminal row with his cariad, slumped at the bar with tears streaking his face and his long fluffy ears drooping disconsolately into his pint. It was heartbreaking. As midnight struck, we whispered 'Happy New Year' to each other and clinked glasses very, very, quietly, before getting the hell out of there by quarter past.

It was time to get back to the *Keewaydin*, and we slid out of New Quay like a stately old dame. Almost immediately, we were straight back in the wilderness again. And it was just perfect. The landscape is vast and craggy, where ancient, massive rocks meet the unyielding force of the ocean. And there can be no better way to see it than from the side of the *Keewaydin*, itself a prize nugget of history. It was a magnificent experience, positively humbling in fact. After all, the beauty of the coast – and the beauty of the boat, it's to be hoped – will still be there long after we've all gone.

If New Quay boldly stares out to sea, proud and unabashed, then Aberaeron seems to shy away, its face barely visible as we glided towards the harbour. Get on land, though, and you'll see that that face has been plastered with as much slap as a six year old let loose with her mother's make-up bag. Houses, pubs and shops are painted in every possible colour, quite often all at once. Although I'm usually firmly in favour of this kind of thing, in Aberaeron it somehow looks a mite contrived, forced even.

But then, that could be just down to my totally irrational dislike of the place. Just as I fell in love with New Quay the first time I met it, so did I not take to Aberaeron on our first encounter, and I've not changed my opinion yet. After the cobbles, curves and characters of New Quay, Aberaeron's all a bit straight and neat and, dare I say, prissy. It's a very beautiful town, a fine example of Georgian planning in all its symmetrical glory, but it doesn't feel like a Welsh seaside town should to me, more like something from New England, or even old England.

To persuade me otherwise, I met up with local architect David Thomas (no relation to the Dylan Thomas author, nor, as far as I know, to Dylan himself). He is a big fan of Aberaeron's undoubtedly remarkable architecture, although he warns against treating it as a time capsule with no room for progress in its visual thinking. We disagreed about the new footbridge over the harbour – I like it, but he thought it too heavy and that something with more grace should have been designed to fly over the water. But I was in total agreement with him about one other hideous recent addition to the townscape, something that really got David quite impassioned. Not a building, but the set of municipal bus stops that had lately erupted along the main street. They're from that off-the-peg Heritage school of design, the same place, I guess, that churns out those ubiquitous black-and-gold bollards and matching bins and benches that every town in the land now sports. Unfortunately, Heritage design only seems to stretch to one age, and that's Victorian Industrial, so the Aberaeron bus stops take their visual cue from railway architecture (in black and gold, of course), and are wholly out of keeping with a Georgian town.

David didn't entirely convince me that Aberaeron was for me, and that feeling wasn't helped when I then dropped my car keys down a drain just as I was locking the door. All in all, it was a curiously low-key end to what had been such a dramatic and spirit-soaring journey. I definitely prefer my Wales on the wild side, and this journey had provided plenty of that.

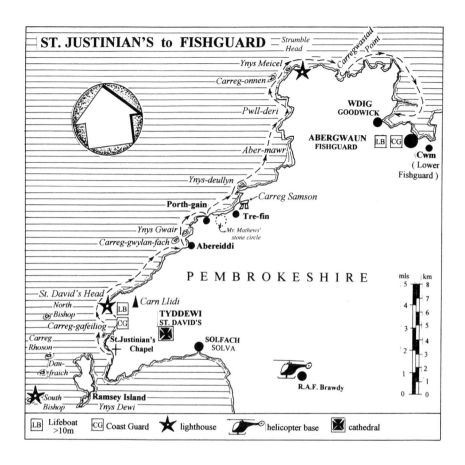

ST. JUSTINIAN'S to FISHGUARD

Strumble Head

Carregwastad Point

Ynys Meicel

Carreg-onnen

Pwll-deri

WDIG
GOODWICK

ABERGWAUN
FISHGUARD

LB CG

Cwm
(Lower
Fishguard)

Aber-mawr

Ynys-deullyn

Carreg Samson

Porth-gain

Tre-fin

Ynys Gwair

Mr. Mathews'
stone circle

Carreg-gwylan-fach

Abereiddi

PEMBROKESHIRE

mls | km
5 — 8
— 7
4 — 6
— 5
3 — 4
— 3
2 — 2
— 1
1 —
0 — 0

St. David's Head

North

Bishop

Carreg-gafeiliog

Carreg-
Rhoson

Dau-
fraich

South
Bishop

Carn Llidi

LB

CG

St.Justinian's
Chapel

TYDDEWI
ST. DAVID'S

SOLFACH
SOLVA

R.A.F. Brawdy

Ramsey Island
Ynys Dewi

| LB | Lifeboat >10m | CG | Coast Guard | ★ | lighthouse | helicopter base | cathedral |

97

CHAPTER EIGHT:
ST JUSTINIAN'S - FISHGUARD
Rib over troubled waters

Everyone has a point on the compass that they're drawn to the most. Mine has always been the west. Wherever I go in the world, the westward pull always kicks in. Part of it is my urge to head for a good sunset – I'm definitely more of a dusk man than a dawn man. But in these islands, west, and to some extent north, are also the compass points of the anti-establishment, and that's part of the appeal too. Just look at a map of Britain and Ireland. At every turn, power, money and authority slides down to the south and east. Each capital city – Dublin, Belfast, Cardiff, Edinburgh and London – is in the east, and usually the south too, of its patch. Give me the free-thinking, often slightly anarchic west, chilling out as the sun goes down, any day. And so we travelled to Wales' westernmost point, just short of St David's Head, but, contrary to my preferred timetable, we had to do it at the crack of dawn.

It was before 6am when I clambered aboard the rib (Rigid Inflatable Boat) that was to take me from St Justinian's, the tiny harbour to the west of St David's. The rib is owned by one of the local pleasure boat companies who ferry thousands of tourists every month around the cliffs, coves, caves and islands of west Pembrokeshire. I've done a couple of the trips before, and they are breathtaking – quite literally, when you're hurtling across the water at breakneck speed. When Helen, the director, Guto, the researcher, and I had been down in the area to recce the programme, we'd gone on one such voyage around Ramsey Island, with commentary from skipper Ffion Rees. She was so good that we asked the company if we could have her guide us up the coast for the programme.

Speed at dawn on the rib

Helen wanted to get some shots of me on board the boat, zooming around the bay, so Ffion, co-skipper Rob Jones and I set off while the crew balanced precariously on another boat to film us rocketing by. After ten minutes of skimming across the water, complete with hair-raising hairpin bends, I was well and truly awake and thoroughly looking forward to the journey. We skimmed back into St Justinian's and picked up the crew.

Little is known about St Justinian, who gave his name to this tiny harbour, home of the St David's lifeboat and our launch pad. Justinian was St David's closest friend and confidante – indeed, their bones are mixed together in one casket in St David's Cathedral. His original resting place is supposed to be here, and the ruins of a chapel mark the spot where, after being decapitated by some of his servants, he is said to have carried his head to. As usually happens in such tales, a spring of pure water welled up on the spot as he placed his severed head on the ground. He wouldn't have to bend down to drink it, either.

The ruined chapel now sits on the neatly-manicured lawns of a house that has become sadly notorious lately. At the time of writing, the house (complete with chapel) is still on the market, with a Gloucestershire estate agent, for a sneeze under £1 million. The controversy that has reigned came about because, when the house was advertised in *The Daily Telegraph* (of course), the ad stated that "the vendors are hoping to sell to a holiday-home owner, rather than a local". Not surprisingly, this had caused huge offence locally, and you can only suppose that that is exactly what the vendor intended. It's even more outrageous when you consider that, as well as the house, he is selling an ancient chapel laden with significance in the rich history of the Welsh saints. Although this particular example of

99

gross insensitivity was, thankfully, a rare exception, the whole thorny issue of holiday homes was something of a dominant theme all the way up this stretch of coast, and we were to come across it again and again.

We'd chosen a rib as the vehicle for this journey for the simple reason that they are so versatile. You can speed them up and slow them down in an instant and, even more importantly, it would give us the chance to get in as close as we liked to the shore, and its abundant wildlife, or even take a trip inside some of the amazing sea caves down this way. But it was a bit of a squeeze – Ffion, Rob, me, Helen, Dave the cameraman and Dafydd the sound man, plus all the equipment packed in tight, as we headed off into the sunrise.

The sun rose perfectly over the rocky, volcanic protrusion of Carn Llidi, the westernmost hill in mainland Wales. It guards St David's Head, that graceful finger of land littered with ancient remains and infused with a power that courses through you when you explore it in the right frame of mind. St David's Head also fulfils another noble function, in that it serves as the boundary between two different areas of the shipping forecast map – we were leaving Lundy and heading into Irish Sea. I adore the shipping forecast. It's the most relaxing thing on the radio, especially when it's read in the husky honey tones of Charlotte Green. Who cares where South Utsire is or whether Channel Light Vessel Automatic is rising, falling or hazy? To us landlubbers, it's all just gorgeous aural hypnotism, dashed with a hint of the heroic and the exotic.

Ffion proved to be the only female skipper that we ever worked with in *Coast to Coast*. I asked her how easy it was to get on as a woman in such a boys' world. "You have to work twice as hard to prove you're half as good," she told me, but she'd never wanted to do anything else. Her dad used to fish professionally, and she'd gone out on the boat with him from an early age, swiftly falling under the sea's powerful spell. Her love for the area shone through everything she said, and her knowledge of it was

With Ffion Rees, our only female skipper

superb.

She told me a great tale about a deserted farmstead, Maes-y-Mynedd, high up on the cliffs, above a seal-filled pebbly cove. It fell into ruin after being abandoned suddenly by a Quaker community who lived from fishing the sea in front of them by stringing a line right the way across the cove and placing hooks from it. They – as people would say these days on the regional tea-time news – "kept themselves very much to themselves", only ever appearing occasionally in St David's to sell their catches. There was a lot of suspicion towards them in the area, and it culminated when a nearby farmer dumped a poisoned dog carcass in their drinking water well, which was the point at which the community disappeared overnight and left their farm to crumble.

On almost every shoreline rock, Atlantic Grey Seals basked and stared us out. "They're as interested in us as we are in them," Ffion told me, and it certainly seemed to be the case. Some of them are born exhibitionists, and loved showing off for their occasional visitors. Bobbing and swirling around them were thousands of sea birds, nowhere near as keen to see us as their cute, blubbery mates. Particularly anti-social are fulmars, which have a very effective way of seeing off unwelcome visitors. They regurgitate the contents of their stomach into a vile-smelling, sticky ooze and then projectile vomit it out at the intruder. What a skill! How useful would that be? You'd never get another Jehovah's Witness knocking on your door with that kind of trick up your sleeve. The seals and birds were set against a backdrop of dazzlingly turquoise water and jagged cliffs of purple and black. It could only be Pembrokeshire.

With so many offshore reefs and rocks, this coast has seen more than its fair share of wrecks and lost lives over the centuries. As well as the danger of the natural terrain, Pembrokeshire, facing square out into the Atlantic and the prevailing south-westerly winds, sees its weather change in minutes flat. "It can be glorious and sunny in the morning and blowing

The old quarry at Abereiddi, now fancifully known as the Blue Lagoon

a gale by lunchtime," Ffion said. Her words were to prove strangely prophetic.

The spooky remains of Abereiddi loomed into view shortly. Pembrokeshire is something of a Wales-in-miniature, with its slate-quarrying, Welsh-speaking north and coal-mining, English-speaking south. Abereiddi was one of the old slate quarries, and when that shut a century ago, the sea wall of the quarry was blasted out, allowing the ocean to flood in. Minerals in the old quarry react with the salt in the water, turning the sea a violent cobalt shade of blue, and earning it the inevitable moniker of the Blue Lagoon. Few boats can get over the shallow lip of the quarry and in to the lagoon, but it was high tide and we were in a zippy little rib, so we purred in with the greatest of ease. The sheer black walls of the old quarry make it quite a dark and intimidating sight from the boat, and I wasn't too sad to leave again and head for Porthgain, just up the coast.

Pembrokeshire slate never attained anything like the quality thresholds of the slate being quarried in northern Wales. In fact, it was of such poor quality that it was hardly ever even used for local house roofs. Most of the older properties locally are roofed with a distinctive look, created by a barbed wire frame over which lime mortar grout is caked, creating a roof that can withstand the Force 8+ gales that batter this coast on at least thirty occasions every winter.

Abereiddi slate had to be shipped out from the beach, as there's no harbour here. Eventually, one was built over the hill at Porthgain, and a tramway constructed to link the two, a few remnants of which you can still see. Porthgain is a perfect natural harbour at the end of a sea creek, and it was still only about 8am as we coursed our way up into it.

Someone I met on this journey described Porthgain as "the only real village left on this coast", and it's easy to see what they meant. The brooding presence of the old brickworks, kiln and quay seem to keep the place rooted in reality, although the relentless march of the art galleries has, of course, made its way down there too. Unlike many other villages hereabouts, there's a high proportion of permanent residents in Porthgain, making for a strong, spirited community that even starred recently in its own Welsh language TV docusoap, *Pobol Porthgain*, the majority of which focussed on the action in the village's deservedly legendary pub, the Sloop Inn.

I've had many fine times in the Sloop over the years. It regularly wins accolades as the best pub in the county, and even a huge development of the place in recent years has just about kept it the right side of wonderful. The food is fabulous, the beer easy and the company always fascinating.

Before the vast Harvester-style room was grafted on to the side, that part of the pub was a small snug, where I watched England being beaten on penalties in the semi-final of Euro '96 by (of course) Germany. Also in the room and glued to the match were a bunch of schoolkids from East Anglia on a geography field trip, their teachers and a German travel writer and his family. The writer was doing an article about Britain for a German magazine, and was also taking photographs to illustrate it. When it came to the dreaded penalty shoot-out, he positioned himself under the TV screen and turned his lens on the school party and me, snapping away at our reaction to every penalty attempt. I never saw his article, but I've got a strong suspicion that it was probably illustrated by a shot of our collective horror as Gareth Southgate missed the vital attempt and consigned England to a few more year's hurt. A fine example of *schadenfreude* from the people that brought us the word.

By the time we reached Porthgain, we'd been up for hours, had sailed an invigorating ten miles or so and it was still only early in the morning. We were ravenous, and fell on the owner of the harbourside cafe as soon as she appeared to open up, like a gang of alcoholics jostling at the pub door for opening time. She coped magnificently, conjuring up endless pots of tea and coffee and mountains of toast and jam.

The cafe is owned by Rob Jones, who'd been our co-skipper from St Justinian's and who was going to take over for the final run into Fishguard, as Ffion had to get back for a day running the guided tourist tours. Rob was one of the real stars of *Pobol Porthgain*, and he was a great source of knowledge of the area.

In a part of the world so prodigiously rocky, the village of Trefin – just inland from Porthgain – shows some fine examples of man putting it to great use. Right on the village green is a rock chair, which is where the village mayor used to be enthroned in a mock coronation, a practice that still took place occasionally as recently as the 1970s, and prime candidate, I would have thought, for a joyful resurrection.

Go west from Trefin and your eyes are drawn to what appears to be a stunning reminder of the ancients in the shape of a stone circle sited high above the cliffs. How many coast path pilgrims have lingered here or even danced naked in the moonlight, unaware that this circle's history stretches back only as far as the 1990s, when it was erected by the local landowner – Cerys Matthews' dad, no less.

I've got to confess that none of us knew this at the time, when Helen, Guto and I first encountered it on the pre-filming recce a couple of weeks before. As we were driving out of Trefin, I spotted the stone circle on the horizon, and it looked amazing. But there was nothing marked on the map, which made me wonder if it was a recent addition. We went to have a look at it, and then knocked on the door of the nearby house. Much to our surprise, a very handsome, twinkling young buck with a southern American drawl came to answer. He said that his father-in-law had built the circle, but he wasn't in right now. "Could we have his phone number and I'll ring and ask him if we can film there?" Helen asked brightly. "Sure," the American replied, smiling, and he went in to write it down for us. Still none of us were any the wiser who he was.

It was only later that night that someone in the pub mentioned Cerys' parents living locally, by a stone circle that her dad had built, did the penny drop. Cerys was, at the time, late on in her pregnancy and the dashing young American was, of course, none other than her husband Seth. They'd married earlier in the year in the little chapel at nearby Square and Compass, famously travelling there by tractor. I was really impressed that he so trustingly handed over their phone number to a passing TV crew. No wonder Cerys wanted to come back to Pembrokeshire to have the baby.

Her parents' house overlooks the ruins of Melin Trefin, the old mill that was immortalised in William Crwys Williams' epic poem of the same name. It had more recently inspired Cerys and Seth – my new friends, as I like to think of them – to name their new daughter Glenys Pearl Y Felin. She's a lucky little mill.

After the less-than-ancient stone circle of Mr Matthews, I was keen to see the real thing, a mile east of Trefin, in the shape of the magnificent Carreg Samson cromlech, or burial chamber. It's around four and a half thousand years old and with a thunderous sixteen by nine foot capstone held up on only three slender points. Mesolithic flint tools have been found here, and it spent many years as a makeshift sheep pen, but now it merely sits and dreams above the rugged coast, and invites you to do the same.

By the time Rob Jones guided us out of Portnhgain harbour in his rib, the weather had done exactly as Ffion described. We'd left St Justinian's in a fabulous sunrise, and clear early morning sunshine had illuminated our way to Porthgain, but, only an hour letter, lumpy great clouds had filled the sky and rain was falling. The sea was no longer a gorgeous turquoise, but an churning steel grey frothed with white spume. Rob was upbeat enough – "oh, we'll be fine" – but I wasn't so sure. He was also pretty upbeat about the holiday home issue, while recognising that villages all the way up this coast are fast becoming little more than empty husks come the winter. But there's an extra twist to the tale in Pembrokeshire, especially when compared with, say, northern or central

Wales, where most of the holiday home owners hail from the north-west and Midlands of England respectively. Most of the *tŷ haf* owners hereabouts hail from south-eastern Wales, particularly from amongst the booming Cardiff professional classes, often Welsh-speaking. The dizzying rise in house prices in the capital has seeped along the M4 westwards, and Pembrokeshire is now one of the most overpriced parts of Wales. Is this a more acceptable form of holiday home ownership? I don't know, but the net effect, of empty houses and dwindling local resources, is much the same.

Visibility was poor as we passed the little creek of Abercastell and headed round to the great sweep of Aber Mawr, one of the few sandy beaches along this coast. Most of the beaches are pure rock and shingle, and even those are in fairly short supply. I hadn't quite realised just how sheer and stark most of this coast was. In many ways, I'd say, the best views are from the 187-mile Pembrokeshire Coast Path, where at least you get the fusion of cliffs and rocks with the gentle green scenery as an antidote to the almost relentless dark severity of the view we were getting.

It was now really bucketing down with rain, though I'd long since passed that level of saturation where you go beyond caring. And I was really excited about seeing the vast, rugged sea cliff near Pwllderi, on the way up to Strumble Head. It's the best part of two miles long, hundreds of feet high and pretty much straight. Suddenly we were right underneath it, a tiny bright blip next to the towering wall of black rock that stretched off far into the cloud and rain. Wisps of mist swirled enigmatically across the rock face, sea birds glided by and still the water poured down. I was wet through, but elated. When you look at a sight like this in these sort of conditions, and it still thrills you to the core, you know that you're a hopeless Wales addict.

The lighthouse at Strumble Head flashed by as we motored on

Not happy in the rain with second skipper Rob Jones

towards Fishguard. It's always struck me that they make such a lot of noise round these parts about what has become known as the Last Invasion of Britain, imbuing it with a gravity and danger it doesn't really warrant. The 1997 bicentenary of the event was celebrated like it was the Battle of Hastings all over again. Truth is, the hopeless Franco-Irish rabble who landed in 1797 proved to be as much threat as a slight headcold. They scrambled ashore and swiftly found themselves capturing a nearby farmhouse, which, thanks to a recent shipwreck and an imminent family wedding, was stuffed to the gunwales with fine food and drink. The would-be conquerors set to the supplies with such relish that they were pissed as newts within hours and unable to threaten anything more than a dormouse. In their drunken confusion, they did manage to raid the church at Llanwnda, nicking a few pewter plates as they went. And that was about as derring-do as they got. Quite honestly, Britain's seen more menacing invasions during the Rugby World Cup or when Madonna moved here. But we stopped all the same to see the place near Carregwastad Point where the invaders landed. If the weather had been half as bad that day as it was when we were there, they'd have turned round and gone home.

Rounding the corner, we caught our first sight of Fishguard and the breakwater that protects the harbour. Or not, as it transpired. It was a huge piece of engineering – over 800 tons of rubble were needed for every foot of its half-mile length – but, according to Rob, the architect got his angles all wrong and built it in the wrong position. Apparently, he was so distraught by his cock-up that he eventually committed suicide.

Sure enough, as we rounded the breakwater, the water, if anything, became even choppier than it had in the open ocean. Docked already was the huge Stena liner bound for Rosslare, and we had to cosy up to its side, a mouse to an elephant, in order to disembark on the quay. It was very hairy. In the conditions, all Rob could do was to steer headlong into the wall, with each one of us having to jump on to the stone steps as we got near. We were all tired, wet and cold, the water was perilously rough and the rain still bucketing down. With only Dafydd, the sound man, left on board, Rob lost position by the steps and was forced to steer towards a zinc ladder running up the quay wall. Dafydd, with his heavy mixer pack round his neck, had to throw himself at the ladder. Just as he got a foothold, a surging wave whipped the boat away and he was left alone at the bottom of a very wet and very long ladder. Dafydd has no head for heights, and we all watched in nervous silence from the quay as he started to haul himself up rung by rung as the rain poured down on him and the swell churned furiously just beneath his feet. It was agonising to watch, but it must have been a nightmare to do. All in a day's work for a sound recordist.

Fishguard, Abergwaun in Welsh, is really three separate towns in one. The westerly section around the port and railway station is, technically, Goodwick. Fishguard town proper is a mile east at the top of a hill. Down on the other side of the hill is Lower Fishguard, or Cwm, gathered prettily around the old harbour.

Like many ports, Fishguard has had to fight hard to be seen as a destination in its own right, rather than just somewhere to pass through as quickly as possible. In some ways, though, this has done the place a favour. Compared with the rather rarefied, distinctly upwardly-mobile settlements elsewhere on the coast, Fishguard feels like a real place, full of real people and with a very appealing, mellow culture fused from its Irish and Welsh influences.

When the port was built in 1907, hopes were high that Fishguard would come to rival Liverpool and Southampton as the launch port for transatlantic voyages. Part of the appeal was a speedy Great Western Railway service direct to London from the Harbour station – so speedy, in fact, that it takes nearly an hour longer to do to the same journey today than it did almost a century ago. In fact, there are no longer any direct trains from Fishguard to London, and there's only two trains a day from here going anywhere, and one of those is at two in the morning. Bizarrely enough, in the summer, the afternoon service from here goes to Cardiff and then up the Rhymney Valley, calling at all stations. Well, who'd want to go to dirty London when you can go straight to Bargoed or Ystrad Mynach?

As a respite from the endless rain, we called in on Steve Roberts at the Hamilton Backpackers Lodge in Fishguard town. Backpackers' hostels are one of the best places to stay on any budget. I've spent months travelling around such places in Ireland, but the phenomenon is pretty new in Wales, and there are still only a few. They are very different from official YHA youth hostels, which generally have far stricter rules, and different again from bunkhouses, which tend to cater for groups. Steve gave us gallons of tea and we sat out and chatted on his covered veranda, me happily ensconced in his hammock-chair amongst sculptures and artwork from all over the world. There's a lovely, relaxed atmosphere about the Hamilton. People often stay for weeks or months, even getting casual work in local pubs just so that they can hang out here a while longer. Backpackers' hostels appeal to independent travellers of all ages and nationalities, although it has to be said that every time we went to the place, there seemed to be a very high proportion of attractive young

Aussie Sheilas. Steve didn't seem to mind.

He's got an interesting old pedigree, Steve. He's the son of one of the first wave of back-to-the-land hippies who arrived in Pembrokeshire in the late sixties. It must be difficult rebelling against such parents. You can't wind your mum and dad up by smoking dope, or having lots of sex, or getting into really awful music, because they've already been there, done that and got the tie-dyed T-shirt. Steve's rebellion took him away for twenty years, travelling the world and, I think, feeling rather rootless. But roots eventually did kick in, and they were for the area that he'd grown up in near Fishguard. Opening a backpackers' hostel there was a logical progression.

I asked him how he feels independent, backpacking tourists are treated in this country. Not very well, was the immediate response, and I heartily agreed. Amongst the tourist board bosses and bureaucrats, the perception is that such people bring very little money into the area, and are thus best ignored. Such an attitude is endemic in Wales, where tourist boards seem to think that the only tourists worth sucking up to are either wealthy golfing Americans or wealthy German misty-eyed Celtic fantasists. Yet today's scruffy Scandinavian backpacker on a tight budget may well be tomorrow's CEO of Volvo, and if s/he remembers a great time had in Wales twenty-five years ago, s/he might just return to spend lots of money in posh hotels and restaurants or even think of us when it comes to opening a new components plant. And even the assumption that independent travellers don't spend cash is way misplaced. Many stay around for weeks or months, spending a steady amount of money on food, drink, transport and entertainment as they do.

Last port of call was Cwm, or Lower Fishguard, and here I was back on my own personal Dylan Thomas trail. Cwm was chosen (much to the chagrin of New Quay and Laugharne) as the location for the blockbuster 1971 film version of *Under Milk Wood*. It's a wonderful movie, as it doesn't

The celluloid Llareggub:
Cwm (Lower Fishguard)

try too hard to stick religiously to the text, which, after all, was written as a radio "play for voices". Instead, it takes the phantasmagoric atmosphere and language of the piece and builds its own visual feast from it. With a glittering cast that included Richard Burton, Elizabeth Taylor, Siân Phillips, Peter O'Toole and Ryan Davies, this was a major production, and a huge event in a tiny community like Cwm.

On the pre-filming recce, we went into Cwm's wonderful old pub, *The Ship*, whose walls are plastered in memorabilia, much of it from the village's brief encounter with celluloid fame. We got chatting with Mary Morley, the pub's exuberant and long-serving barmaid. When she let slip that she had appeared in the film as a child extra, I knew that I wanted to talk to her on camera. She was fantastic as she spilled some of the gossip from thirty-odd years ago, including the great nugget that Liz Taylor had never actually come to film in Fishguard, but had insisted on doing all her scenes (as Polly Garter) in the studio far away. Off camera, one of the other regulars in the bar told me how Richard Burton had been overheard bawling down the phone at her in the foyer of the stately old Fishguard Bay Hotel in Goodwick, where the film crowd were all based. At one point he is said to have hollered "look, just get your fat arse down to Fishguard!" She never did.

Best of the memorabilia is a plaque that the film crew had inscribed for the pub proprietors. It solemnly records that:

THIS IS TO CERTIFY THAT THE SHIP STAYED OPEN OFFICIALLY
FROM FRIDAY 19TH 1700 HOURS TO SATURDAY 20TH 0500
TO SATISFY THE THIRST OF THE FILM UNIT,
IN WHICH THEY FAILED MISERABLY.

Again, the stories I was told off camera were even better. One bloke told me how his dad, who ran a taxi firm of seven vehicles, was personally ascribed to Burton for the duration of the filming, twenty four hours a day and seven days a week. Part of his job was to keep a bootful of gin, which he would be required to top Burton up with whenever he demanded it, including first thing in the morning. The director of the movie, Andrew Sinclair, has since gone on record as saying that they had to be very sparing with close-ups of Richard Burton, as his eyes were generally so badly bloodshot from those gins. Someone in the pub also claimed to have regularly scored acid for the cast and crew. If you've seen the movie, you can believe it.

As I knew all too well, Pembrokeshire weather changes on a sixpence, and by the time we'd emerged from *The Ship*, a beautiful summer's evening was breaking out like a sudden smile. As the sun emerged, so did the locals to mess about on the water, from the Celtic longboat crew to the boys of the lifeboat. But I was still firmly under milk wood, watching the day dissolve over the huddle of houses and the boat-bobbing sea. Evening was beckoning, and I looked forward to the chance to be a very Nogood Boyo indeed.

The journey had lived up to all my expectations of savage beauty, but, after a week in northern Pembrokeshire, I was left feeling faintly and unspecifically saddened. On the surface, the communities of the area looked as trim and beguiling as ever, but rampant gentrification – as evidenced by the relentless march of chi-chi eateries and art galleries, some great but too many full of winsome, insipid watercolours – told its own tale. I felt like asking, would the real northern Pembrokeshire, wild, untamed and fiercely individual, please stand up?

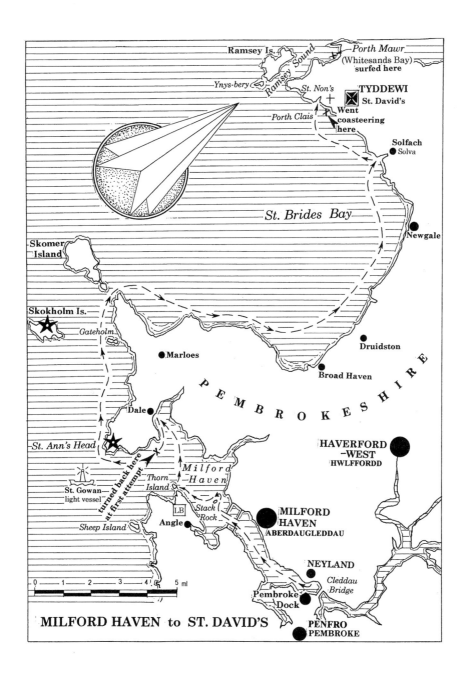

Ramsey Is.
Porth Mawr
(Whitesands Bay)
surfed here

Ynys-bery

Ramsey Sound

St. Non's

TYDDEWI
St. David's

Went
coasteering
here

Porth Clais

Solfach
Solva

St. Brides Bay

Newgale

Skomer Island

Druidston

Skokholm Is.

Gateholm

Marloes

Broad Haven

Dale

P E M B R O K E S H I R E

St. Ann's Head

HAVERFORD -WEST HWLFFORDD

turned back here at first attempt

Milford Haven

Thorn Island

St. Gowan light vessel

LB

Stack Rock

MILFORD HAVEN ABERDAUGLEDDAU

Sheep Island

Angle

NEYLAND

Cleddau Bridge

0 — 1 — 2 — 3 — 4 5 ml

Pembroke Dock

MILFORD HAVEN to ST. DAVID'S

PENFRO PEMBROKE

CHAPTER NINE:

MILFORD HAVEN - ST DAVID'S
Next Stop America

This was the very first *Coast to Coast* that we filmed, in early July 2002. With none of us knowing quite how to do it, and finding ourselves utterly at the mercy of elements that often refused to play ball, we ended up filming loads more than we could ever possibly squeeze into a half hour programme. It was a very busy week.

The journey, from Milford Haven to St David's, felt like a pilgrimage from Mammon to God. Milford Haven is a strange town, with a very strange history, but it's a place I've always instinctively liked. Its unique pedigree starts with the fact that it was born, just over two centuries ago, out of a salacious, celebrity love triangle – and there's not many towns you can say *that* about. In the late eighteenth century, the land bordering the Milford Haven waterway, a glittering gash of deep sea thrust through the soft hills of south Pembrokeshire, was owned by Sir William Hamilton. His nephew, Charles Frances Greville, was heavily in debt and betrothed to one Emma Hart. In an apparently straight swap, Hamilton cancelled Greville's debts and employed him to build and manage the town of Milford Haven, while he took up with his nephew's pneumatic sweetheart, whom he made Lady Hamilton. To further spice the stew, she, of course, then became the celebrated mistress of Lord Nelson, even bearing him a daughter condemned to suffer under the name Horatia. And some folk would like to have us believe all this sort of carry-on was invented in the 1960s.

Nelson visited the new town of Milford Haven in 1802, and the inn where he stayed (and where he dined, it's to be hoped cheerfully, with his lover, her husband and her ex) was promptly renamed in his honour. The Lord Nelson (now with Emma's nightclub – of course – at its rear) is still there today, occupying one of the largest Georgian houses on the town's most elegant thoroughfare, Hamilton Terrace, the lower of three grand parallel terraces cascading down to the Haven's edge. This spacious, gracious approach to town planning is rare in the higgledy-piggledy world of Welsh settlements, and it still impresses today. Perhaps inevitably, the swankier houses on Hamilton Terrace – those enlivened with a little touch of New England in the shape of a wrought iron veranda, for instance – are now mostly banks and solicitors' offices.

Not that Milford Haven is awash with money. Far from it. In its short life of just two hundred years, the town has seen the rise and decline of no less than three successive staple industries, and its citizens are no nearer idle luxury for any of them. First, there were the by-products of whaling, from corsets and perfumes to the highly lucrative sperm whale oil that was lighting the streets of Georgian cities, at least until gas took over in the 1820s and the Milford industry promptly died. Decades of struggle ensued as the town made vainglorious bids to establish itself as a transatlantic port (only one lonely liner ever docked here, in 1898). The spanking new docks, however, provided space abundant for the fishermen and women who flocked here from all over Wales, England and Scotland, giving the town a cosmopolitanism still evident today. Even with a vast stock of such natural resources as fish, permanent stability proved, once again, elusive. Arguments about over-fishing surfaced before World War I, but little was heeded, and the Milford fishing trade became a victim of its own success. And greed. 59,000 tonnes of the "silver darlings" were caught in the peak year of 1946, after lesser activity during the second world war had enabled the fish to thrive, but a decade later, the catch was down to 22,500 tonnes and, before long, to a steadyish 10,000 tonnes a year. Seagulls still squawk hopefully around the few remaining trawlers and there's still an ice factory on the docks, but fishing is very much a secondary industry these days.

For Milford Haven is now an oil town. Horizons in all directions are dominated by the *Mad Max*-like refineries, blotting out the landscape like overgrown chemistry sets. The superb local museum, in the old Customs House on the docks, makes a brave play at calling this the "second oil age", harking back to the whale oil that drove the town's foundation two centuries ago. But crude oil, shipped in tankers quarter of a mile long, is a very different beast to the homespun whaling industry. This is corporate megabucks, one of the world's most powerful industries alighting on this corner of Pembrokeshire out of pure expediency (the Haven being a perfect deep water inlet for its vast tankers). These leviathans, higher than twenty-storey buildings, dock at Brobdingnagian private jetties, screened away by razor wire and guard dogs from their host town. The town and the tankers co-exist because they have to, but there is little real interchange or mutual goodwill.

How small the people of Milford Haven feature in the thinking of the oil barons was graphically, painfully illustrated in February 1996, when the Texaco tanker, *Sea Empress*, ran aground off nearby St Ann's Head. The Liberian-registered vessel, with its Russian crew and Cypriot captain, was left to founder on the rocks for nine days before being towed into port. By then, 73,000 tonnes of crude oil had slimed and glooped its way along the Welsh coast, devastating 35 Sites of Special Scientific Interest, a unique coastal ecology (and National Park) and killing at least 20,000 seabirds. During the crisis, sirens hollered, helicopters swooped overhead, St Ann's Head was closed at gunpoint and local people were breathing air that *tasted* of petrol, but little information or compensation was ever forthcoming.

The oil slick from the *Sea Empress* wasn't the only unpleasant unguent to have washed up on the shores of Milford Haven. A florid ten-foot memorial stone by the docks bridge commemorates how George IV, that most louche of all British kings (and there's some stiff competition for *that* title), was stranded here twice in three days trying to reach Ireland, thanks to some typically inclement weather out at sea, or, as the memorial has it, "violent and succeeding tempests". It goes on to note that the king "landed by the adjacent steps at Milford cheered by continued acclamations and shouts of welcome from thousands of His Majesty's loyal and warm-hearted Welsh subjects". It's hard to imagine the portly, indulgent monarch, seasick and thoroughly naffed off with being unable to reach the high life in Dublin, managing to respond in kind.

When we set out from neighbouring Neyland Marina, I was desperately hoping that I wouldn't be following His Majesty's example. Conditions in the sheltered natural harbour of the Haven were pretty choppy, and that meant that it could well be near gale force once we got around St Ann's Head and into the open ocean. Our boat was the *Predator*, skippered by local lad Kevin John, who normally takes divers out to explore the hundreds of wrecks in and around the Milford Haven.

Often, you go to a place and just about everyone you meet will trot out the same facts and figures about their locale, as if they've all been on a council-sponsored training day to wow the visitors. In Milford, the one fact that everyone kept reminding us of was that the Milford Haven waterway is the second largest natural harbour in the world, after Sydney in Australia. Seeing the Haven that grey morning made me think. Sydney has the Opera House and the magnificent Harbour Bridge (as well as almost limitless sunshine). Milford has oodles of refineries and the 1970s functionalism of the Cleddau Bridge. It didn't feel like much of a comparison.

Kevin cosied up close to a couple of the nineteenth century fortifications dotted around the Haven. These became known as Palmerston Follies, after the Prime Minister of the day, and were a huge programme of fortification of Britain's western coasts in anticipation of an attack by the post-revolutionary French under Napolean. The scheme, which nearly bankrupted the country, saw no less than fourteen massive fortifications built in the Milford Haven alone. Some are gone, some are ruinous, one is an upmarket Landmark Trust holiday cottage, one a Field Studies Centre, a few are lost within the refineries and the remainder are in private hands. We circled around one of the latter, Stack Rock, an island fortress that is terrifyingly squat and massive when you get up close to it. A businessman bought the place for £25,000 a few years ago and has so far done nothing with it.

There are big plans afoot however for another of the island fortresses from this era. Thorn Island, just off West Angle Bay, spent years as a cult hotel before closing its doors in the mid 1990s. It is destined to become a hotel once again, this time with a cable car linking it to the mainland a few hundred yards away. Having landed at Thorn Island, I can see why the cable car is integral to the plans. Kevin anchored the *Predator* in the bay and took Emyr, the cameraman and director, Dafydd, the sound man, and me in his dinghy to the bottom of the stone steps that lead up to the island's buildings. As the sea rose and fell beneath us, we basically just had to throw ourselves at the barnacle-covered rock and cling on for dear life. And then he buggered off and left us. It felt like arriving at Alcatraz.

There was something deeply spooky about Thorn Island. The huge, noisy colony of herring gulls that live and breed there really didn't appreciate our intrusion and made no bones about letting us know. Vast tankers slid eerily by and the thick, stone walls of the fort looked cold and impenetrable. I don't think I'll be booking my two week summer break there quite yet.

We crossed the mouth of the Haven to take a look at Dale, the last stop before rounding St Ann's Head. The water's always unusually calm here as this is one of the few east-facing bays in Pembrokeshire, well-hidden from the prevailing westerlies. Combine that with the fact that Dale claims to have more hours of sunshine than any other Welsh village, and it's easy to see why it's a mecca for yachting, sailing and windsurfing.

A quick stop for lunch and Emyr wanted to get some pictures of Kevin and I coming into Dale on board the boat. Em and Dafydd set up on the beach, while Kev and I chugged in towards the pontoons. The idea was that I'd lean over the side and lasso a rope around one of the mooring bollards, the way proper sailors do. Suffice to say that we tried it about five times – back out to sea, turn round, come in again, me throwing the rope – and I missed every time. Kevin was laughing so hard, he could barely steer.

Abandoning that idea, we picked Emyr and Dafydd up and headed out towards St Ann's Head. The moment we were out of the shelter of Dale Bay, things started to get kind of rough. The weather was still grey and damp, and the swell of the sea was building considerably. "Better than Alton Towers, this," Kevin grinned with an evil cackle. Just a couple of miles from the country's sunniest spot, this south-western tip of Pembrokeshire is the windiest place in Wales, a bleak, invigorating headland that demands respect. When Kevin said that he wasn't prepared to risk going around St Ann's Head and out into open ocean, I was only too happy to agree, and we set off back down the Milford Haven for Neyland.

We had to wait the best part of a week for conditions suitable enough to get us out to sea. In the meanwhile, we'd been down in Monmouthshire, filming the Chepstow to Newport journey. Thus it was that we docked in Newport late one evening, and then had to drive right across southern Wales to arrive in Milford well after midnight for a 4am start the following morning. I wasn't happy, and moaned like a stuck pig to anyone who'd care to listen.

But, my god, it was worth it. As we cruised out of Neyland, the sun started to rise, and the Haven presented an entirely different face to the one we'd seen the previous week. The water was glassy smooth and even the refineries, in the early morning summer sunshine, looked fabulous. Finally clearing St Ann's Head, we emerged into St Bride's Bay, that great chunk bitten out of Pembrokeshire's west coast. To get into the inlets at Solva and St David's, we needed to hit high tide smack on, hence the early start.

Our sleeplessness, however, did result in one nasty injury. Kevin had repeatedly warned us about falling into the open-mouthed hold in the middle of the boat, but it was a warning that passed Emyr by as he was filming me gazing over the side of the boat. One second I was looking at him and the camera, the next they'd both vanished. A roar of pain came up from below. Emyr, his face a distinct shade of puce, had gouged a great chunk out of his shin, which was bleeding profusely. Some elementary First Aid later, he was strapped up and, ever the consummate professional, more concerned that the camera plug into which the sound mixer fed had buckled in the fall. Fortunately, there's an in-built microphone on the camera for use in emergency, and we were able to continue using just that. Emyr, however, has a permanent reminder of *Coast to Coast* in the shape of a scar on his shin, even today.

If the Milford Haven was the hors d'oeuvre to our journey, St Bride's Bay, and its spectacular cliffs, sandy beaches and offshore islands, was the most delicious main course. It looked magnificent, from the stunning rocks of Marloes Sands to the hairy stretch of water, Jack Sound, that separates Skomer from the mainland. No wonder this is Britain's only coastal National Park.

Before long, we were passing one of my favourite Pembrokeshire beaches at Druidston Haven, scene of one of strangest shipwrecks ever seen. In 1791 a boat named the *Increase of Scarborough* ran ashore here. As would happen at such times, locals ran down to the beach to see what they could salvage from the floundering ship. Unfortunately, the *Increase* was carrying a cargo of gunpowder, and some metal that was thrown from the wreck struck a stone on the beach and ignited it. Eight people died in the explosion.

Druidston is a much more peaceful place these days. High above the cliffs is the Druidston Hotel, without doubt one of the most laid-back and cheery in all of Wales. Just next door is the oddest house in the area, the eco-friendly holiday home of Labour MP Bob Marshall-Andrews. With its turf roof and curving shape, it's become known locally as the Teletubby House, which is doubly appropriate really. After all, to want to be an MP, you've got to be pretty Laa-Laa.

A couple of miles north of Druidston saw us chugging along the popular surf beach of Newgale. This is the western end of an invisible, but very potent, boundary, known as the Landsker Line, that separates English-speaking southern Pembrokeshire from the Cymraeg-speaking north of the county. Some sixteen castles are placed along its line to police this border, from Roch, just inland from Newgale, right the way across to Laugharne in southern Carmarthenshire.

It struck me how odd the whole concept of the "Little England beyond Wales" of southern Pembrokeshire must have been for travellers in years gone by. Leaving England, they'd have journeyed through a couple of hundred miles of mountainous, monoglot Welsh-speaking Wales before coming out all this way to find a pocket where only English was spoken. The Landsker Line is still pretty much in evidence today, which is why south Pembrokeshire remains very popular with those kind of English holidaymakers and in-migrants who love the beauty of the Welsh landscape, but who have absolutely no truck whatsoever with the culture that shaped it. More fool them. We never managed to cover the very southern tranche of Pembrokeshire, from Castlemartin, through Tenby and Saundersfoot, to Pendine and Laugharne in *Coast to Coast*. Visually, it would have been awesome, I'm sure, but I find the *Daily Mail* attitudes of many of its inhabitants pretty aggravating, and it wasn't too hard to resist.

More than any other settlement on this coast, the approach to Solva, or Solfach, is far more beautiful and dramatic by sea. Arriving by car just doesn't compare – you can't even see the sea from the road. Creeping quietly into the creek that leads to the harbour early on a summer's morning just took our collective breath away. All around was still and quiet and the dazzling, intense light looked good enough to eat. This was Pembrokeshire at its most magical.

Arriving in Solva harbour on a stunning summer's morning

One of the prettiest and most popular villages on the Pembrokeshire coast, Solva's recent history can be summed up by two of its most famous musical sons. Until thirty years ago or so, the village was a very Welsh seafaring community, linked umbilically to the ocean and its roots in Cymraeg-speaking northern Pembrokeshire. Out of that era came Meic Stevens, Wales' own Bob Dylan, whose songs of protest and agitation, of love and loss, perfectly reflect those turbulent times.

In recent decades, the village has been massively anglicized. Its cute appearance and location on a spectacular stretch of coast have led to a huge influx of well-to-do English, German and other incomers. Where once the streets were full of chandlers and ropemakers, now they're crammed with twee artists' galleries and upmarket restaurants. And out of that stew came David Gray, the soulful white boy who provided the soundtrack to a million middle-class thirtysomething dinner parties in the shape of his mega-selling album, *White Ladder.*

We couldn't hang around too long in Solva, as we needed to get into Porth Clais, the old port to St David's, and that's only possible at high tide. So it was back out to sea again. From there, the St David's peninsula looks pretty forbidding. Punctuating the sheer cliffs are a succession of tiny bays, such as St Non's, where a gloomy religious retreat house squats on the cliffs. St Non was the mother of St David, and this is supposedly the place where the patron saint was born in the middle of a howling storm.

Porth Clais is the tiniest, narrowest of gashes that cut into these cliffs, where the river Alun flows out into the turquoise sea. Narrow and shallow it may be, but it has served as the main port to St David's for fifteen centuries. It's hard to imagine just how many thousands of pilgrims must have landed here, each bursting with hope, faith and expectation of the area's famous magic. As we motored gently up towards the harbour wall, past the purple rocks that were quarried to build St David's Cathedral, the tide was dropping and we had just a few inches to spare. We just made it.

Like learning to swim or losing your virginity, you don't forget your first time in Tyddewi, St David's. In today's travel writing world, words like "magical" and "enchanting" are much over-used, but St David's really is both. Britain's smallest city, tucked away at Wales' westernmost point, breathes a simple and uplifting spirituality, something most noticeable in the stunning cathedral.

These days, St David's seems about as far out on a limb as mainland Wales can possibly provide. Fifteen hundred years ago, however, when the sea was the main thoroughfare for travel and the links between the Celtic lands on the western seaboard of Europe were at their strongest, St

The medieval misericord of some poor soul being seasick in St David's Cathedral

David's would have been the Birmingham New Street of its day, positively humming with pilgrims and traders alike. And it still has an air of importance way, way beyond its size.

The cathedral is, without doubt, the finest in Wales. So much more the surprise, therefore, when you first arrive here and can't even see it. Bemused tourists have been known to point at the Victorian Tabernacl chapel on Goat Street and ask if *that's* the building that they've come all this way to see. For the cathedral is tucked away below the city streets, the reason being that it had to be sited here to keep invaders – who would invariably come by boat – at bay. I've always wondered just how true that can be. Can you really build a church this big that can't be seen from the sea – a sea, I might add, that surrounds it on three sides and is only a mile or so away? Well, yes. Having arrived by boat, I could finally put the story to the test, and it's all true.

St David's Cathedral is the very heart of Welsh spirituality, and you can feel the weight of the ages in the place. Whatever your beliefs, this is the most fabulous place for quiet contemplation and for getting a sense of perspective on our short tenancy of this mortal coil. There are also some fabulous touches of earthy Welsh humour in the cathedral, especially in the choir. Underneath the seats are some amazing carved misericords, each one a kind of medieval cartoon. One shows a raucous wild boar hunt, another someone being swallowed by a monster and my favourite has some poor soul being very graphically seasick. I know just how he feels.

One of the unique aspects of St David's is that this is the only cathedral in all of Britain where the Queen is automatically a member of the cathedral Chapter. Until very recently, there used to be a little cardboard sign adorning the Monarch's Stall which said "Reserved for the Sovereign", making it sound as if she might just pop in unannounced to rest her weary feet after a hard trawl round Kwik Save. I mentioned this in the *Rough Guide* and was disappointed on this visit to see that the sign had now gone. So I sat in Her Majesty's seat instead, and very comfortable it was too.

I've been coming regularly to St David's for well over a decade now, and, even in that short space of time, the place has changed enormously. Property prices have gone through the roof, the surf scene has become all-encompassing and trendy wine bars, straight out of Pontcanna, are mushrooming. The changes were most graphically illustrated to me one morning when I left the B&B we were staying in to go and get a newspaper. With my mind in neutral, I bounded into the shop on the main square that, last time I'd been in town, had been a great little newsagent and general store. I was yards inside before I skidded to a halt and looked around for the first time. Instead of copies of the *Mirror* and *The Western Mail*, I saw pottery and candle holders. Gone was the smell of bacon croissants, to be replaced by that faintly sickly, vaguely New Age gift shop aroma of wax and perfume. Well, you can see the need. There's only about a dozen other commercial gifty galleries in St David's. You never know when you might run out of healing crystals.

I can't quite believe how much of a religion surfing has become in recent years, and Pembrokeshire is fast soaring up the believers' charts. And it's not just surfing – the area is famous for all manner of outdoor pursuits, and I was eager to try one that originated here. Coasteering, as freelance outward bound instructor Gambo told me, is "an adventurous activity involving rocks and the sea, and the very slender area where they meet." In other words, you don a wetsuit, a crash helmet and a buoyancy aid and then leap off rocks into the swell, swim to the next rock, scramble up it and then do it all again. There must be easier ways of getting round the coast.

Gambo and four of his mates took me down to St Non's for our go at coasteering. It was late in the day and the weather had turned pretty grim. An incessant drizzle blew in from the sea as we clambered down to the water's edge. It was an amazing experience, a total adrenaline rush. But I'm not great with heights, and when Gambo's crew gathered on top of a rock, a good twenty-five feet above a tiny inlet that we could barely see, and said that we were going to jump in, I balked at the prospect. To be honest, if it hadn't been for the fact that it was being filmed, I don't think I'd have plucked up the courage to do it. So, when Emyr asked me to go round and do it again so that he could film it from a different angle, for the one and only time in all the filming, I told him to stuff it. Or rather two words that mean much the same thing.

Dreaming of a warm cuppa as I try coast-eering.

Gambo takes out all sorts of groups and parties coasteering. It's particularly popular for those kind of team-building works outings, as it does require considerable trust, courage and a reliance on your fellow coasteerers. The image of a load of bank managers bounding around the rocks and high-fiving each other in the waves hung heavy – and slightly scary – in my brain.

Having got the taste for Pembrokeshire sea water, I was well up for drinking a few more pints of the stuff, so Gambo and his gang took me up to Whitesands Bay for a spot of surfing. Whitesands is the best-known of local surf beaches, and is nearly always fairly busy these days. I'd brought along my trusty boogie board, which they all found pretty funny and before long, I was forced on to a proper surfboard. But not for long. I think the best I managed was a couple of seconds before toppling once more into the sea.

Amongst the gang were two young brothers who were convinced that all this waterborne activity must surely make them irresistible to the ladies, though there was no concrete evidence of this. Much more interestingly, their mum fed us rejuvenating cups of hot chocolate from the back of her camper van as we came ashore. You can really see the appeal of the surf scene – that combination of pulse-quickening adrenaline, the harnessing of nature's power, fresh air, crashing surf and great camaraderie make for a pretty heady mix. Occasionally, it gets a bit up itself (I was recently in Cornwall, and there are beaches there that are virtually out-of-bounds to anyone but the worst posers), but it made for a perfect end to a wonderful journey. For breathtaking beauty and a sheer sense of fun, Pembrokeshire's pretty hard to beat. The secret may be out, but as it accounts for nearly a quarter of the Welsh coastline, there's plenty to go round.

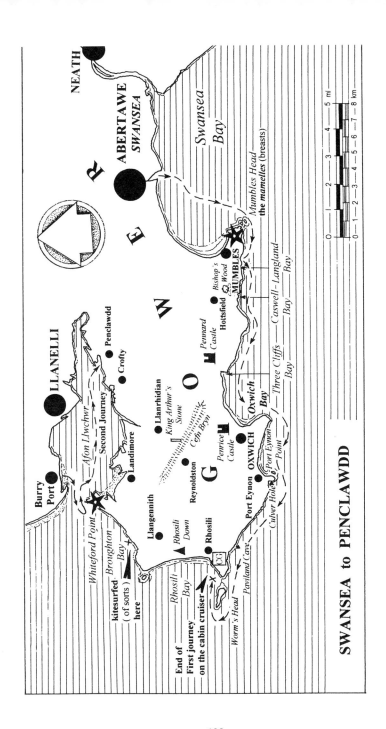

SWANSEA to PENCLAWDD

CHAPTER TEN

SWANSEA - PENCLAWDD
A gin palace & tonic

Of all the twelve programmes, our luxury cruise around Gower was possibly the biggest laugh of the lot. We had such a lot of fun preparing and filming it. For generations, Gower has been one of Wales' favourite playgrounds, and we did all we could to get into the right mood, by working hard at playing hard. As it's a peninsula, we were going to be able to look at Gower from three sides, which gave us the perfect opening for the programme high up on Cefn Bryn, the upland backbone running down its middle. For once, it was possible actually to see almost all the journey we were to undertake from one spot, and, feeling like Jools Holland wandering around his studio introducing his musical turns, it gave me the chance to walk and talk the viewer through what they were about to see.

Our boat was waiting for us in Swansea's legoland Marina. I've got a lot of time for this town. Second cities in any country always have a bit of a chip on their shoulder, and Swansea – like Birmingham, Glasgow, Derry or Cork – is no exception. It's one of the reasons I love it, for that chip gives Swansea its bite and its absolute lack of pretension. If you get a bit la-di-la in Cardiff, chances are someone will give you a grant for it. Try it here, and you'll get laughed out of town. And, unlike in Cardiff, if you hear someone speaking Welsh in Swansea, it doesn't necessarily mean that they've got to be a teacher, an Assembly bureaucrat or a media tart. They might actually be a real person speaking a real language.

When we were planning the second series in Cwmni Da's offices in

Caernarfon, I put in an impassioned plea that, just once, it would be good to have a little wallow in some luxury. Rusty old trawlers and dredgers, stinking of diesel and wet tarpaulin, were all well and good, but we were trying to show the full gamut of both the Welsh coast and the boats that sail around it, and it would be criminal dereliction of duty not to find ourselves at least one floating gin palace. Gower seemed like an appropriate match for such a boat, so Guto the researcher was despatched to find me my luxury cruiser. To that end, he hung rather suspiciously around plush marinas and tried chatting up anyone that looked as if they had an AmEx Platinum Card. It worked.

I arrived at the Marina, having been told to look for the biggest boat of the lot. Across the tangle of bobbing masts, I spotted one that seemed head and shoulders above the rest. And it was ours. I was thrilled. Skippered by Pete Letheren, we were joined by proud owners Bob and Val McHarg, who had made their cash in car sales and caravan parks before ploughing a large wadge of it into the sixty foot beauty I was now boarding. With three bedrooms, a dining room, living area, kitchenette, upper viewing balcony and deck, the *Passage West* was about the size of a terraced house, and probably cost more than the entire street.

Our modest boat for the journey

To complete the crew, we were accompanied as far as Mumbles by self-declared Virtual Mayor of Swansea and all-round local legend, Paul Durden. He is perhaps best known as the author of cult Swansea movie *Twin Town*, the film that brought Rhys Ifans to the attention of the world. Although it never quite recouped its full costs, *Twin Town* is, Durden told me, technically the most successful Welsh film ever. And what a movie it is: fast, filthy and very, very funny.

Durden is also the man who, when Swansea was the UK City of Literature in 1995, won the competition to come up with an updated version of Swansea-born Dylan Thomas' famous epithet for the city, which he so meticulously called an "ugly, lovely town". Unfortunately, Durden's unbeatable winning entry – "pretty shitty city" – fell foul of the competition's sponsors, Marks & Spencer, who promptly pulled the plug on the whole thing. They were obviously hoping for something a little more fragrant – but, for god's sake, this is Swansea. It doesn't *do* fragrant. 1995, the year of the literature beano, was a good year for the old town and has left its mark in the shape of what originally was called Tŷ Llên, the (national) House of Literature, but which, with a certain sense of inevitability, has subsequently been renamed the Dylan Thomas Centre. This will go nicely with the city's Dylan Thomas Theatre, Dylan Thomas Bookshop, Dylan Thomas Festival, Dylan Thomas Square, and Dylan Thomas Birthplace. Why not just rename the bloody city Llanddylan? Mind you, I suppose it's better than naming everything after the city's other favourite prodigal of the moment, Mrs Michael Douglas. Croeso i Zetaville.

If Dylan came back from the grave now, I suspect he'd be flabbergasted (but supremely ego-flattered) about how much is made out of him these days. When I visited his boathouse at Laugharne, the thing that surprised me was how minor a literary figure he was when he was alive. The museum exhibits two newspapers reporting his death. The *Daily Mirror* manages a tiny paragraph on page five, while even the local *Carmarthen Journal* relegates the story to second place behind the tale of a missing farmer.

As we were gliding out of Swansea Marina, Paul made no bones about how much he disliked the development. "There used to be a fish market down here, until the council levelled it and then built this bog-standard marina. Virtually everywhere's got one much the same these days. Now, they don't even let fishing boats in – I mean, they might smell of fish or something and we couldn't have that."

Swansea looks mighty impressive from the sea, in a way that few cities would, thanks to the sharp gradients that make up the city. Draped dramatically around its bay – fancifully likened to the Bay of Naples by some – it all seems in perfect proportion in a way that it rarely does when you're snarled up in the traffic. Paul, however, has his doubts about his native town's status. "Swansea's not a real city, mun – it's a town that thinks it's a city" he said. "It can't be – the most essential thing for a real city to have is a proper red light area. I mean, we've got a few massage parlours, but nothing like you find in Cardiff, say, where there are whole streets full of hookers." But even he has to admit that the city, stretching from the mouth of the Tawe right round to Mumbles, looks pretty good from out here.

A sort of Coney Island to Swansea's New York, Mumbles is the place where second city folk, and many from the western Valleys as well, come to let their hair down. The Mumbles Mile has long been Wales' most famous pub crawl, the pier and seafront provide all the arcades you could need and, these days, Mumbles is fast becoming southern Wales' culinary capital, where swish new cafe-bars and eateries are springing up alongside rococo shops. It's a place custom-built for a good time – no surprise really, when you consider that the name Mumbles derives from the French word, 'mamelles', or breasts, which is what the original settlers saw when they looked at the two little islands off Mumbles Head. On our glinting cruiser, we were heading straight towards them, and I know I'm no expert, but I couldn't see the resemblance myself. They must have had a pretty fertile imagination. Either that, or just a one-track mind. Paul's theory about the derivation of the name Mumbles is that it's a mishearing of Grumbles, something he claims goes on a lot in that corner of the world.

The 'mamelles' (breasts) that gave Mumbles its name. Are there normally three?

Paul was ferried to shore at Mumbles, while we continued around the headland in our turbo-charged floating palace. This is where Gower proper starts, and it was looking good. Statistics abound when it comes to talking about Gower. This solid limb of land, thrust out from southern Wales into the sea, feels at times more like an island than a peninsula, so distinctive is its terrain and atmosphere and so independently-minded are its inhabitants. It reminded me of the French term for a peninsula, *une presqu'île*, or nearly-island, and it sure fits Gower. The statistic that's most often trotted out round here is that Gower was the very first designated Area of Natural Beauty in all of Britain, one of those state-sponsored labels that kind of means everything and nothing at the same time. But the stat that does it for me reflects Gower's history as a feudal society. Although large swathes of the land are still owned by a few aristocratic families, the flip side of the arrangement is that almost half of Gower is common land, where herds of wild sheep, cows and horses roam over the moors and roads entirely impervious to men and motors. And just as it is for the four-legged, so it is for those of us with only two. Gower is just fifteen miles long by five miles wide, and yet within that there are over four hundred miles of public rights of way criss-crossing the landscape. There's a real democracy at work down here, and it's very refreshing to see.

Emyr Jenkins, the director and cameraman for the programme, was at university in Swansea and spent many years living on Gower. In fact, it became something of a running joke that, whichever road we drove down during our week in the area, chances are Emyr would say at some point "see that house? I used to live there". But it was a real treat to have someone who knows the place so well with us, and we spent a good part of our time there sampling fine beer in out-of-the-way pubs and walking some of the lesser-known paths that he remembers so well.

During the week we were filming on Gower, we were all staying in a cottage in Reynoldston, a village scattered across the moorland under Cefn Bryn. Sheep and horses graze contentedly on the tufty village green, and every house drive way has a cattle grid to keep them from wandering in and chewing the herbaceous borders. It was a delightful spot, helped by the fact that we were but a two minute stumble from the *King Arthur's Hotel*, one of Gower's best pubs.

Back on the boat, we passed the last couple of coves before the main roads peter out into the winding lanes of deepest Gower. Langland Bay, backed by its period piece beach huts, is dominated by a turreted mock castle, built as the lavish beach villa of Merthyr Tydfil ironmaster Richard Crawshay. His treatment of his workforce was notoriously harsh, and there's some sweet irony that his seaside retreat went on to become a convalescent home for miners.

Next up was Caswell Bay, also once a venue for busloads of daytripping Valleys miners, and still a hugely popular spot. Few of the hundreds of people who fill the car park on a sunny day turn the other way, however, and wander into the deliciously cool and leafy Bishop's Wood nature reserve. Its warden is Dai Morris, who has added to the wooden sculpture dotted around with a stupendous medieval turf-roofed roundhouse as the hub of the reserve. It's the finest type of art, one that combines grace and beauty with hard-nosed practicality, for the roundhouse is open to all and hosts public events every month. Despite its meaty appearance and proportions, not one nail or screw was used in securing the beams and struts of local timber – everything has been fixed into place using hand-scored dowels and pegs. Dai is obviously – and rightly – very proud of what he described as his "labour of love".

Next time you're stuck in traffic on the commuter run, swearing at the radio warnings to avoid the very spot you're taking root in, think of Dai. He works next to the beach in the nature reserve, and lives at its other end in the famous chalet community of Holtsfield. His journey to work is a bucolic stroll through the woods that takes all of about fifteen minutes. I was eager to do something in the programme about Holtsfield, a place that I'd heard much about when its story hit the front pages back in the early 1990s. One of the unique features of Gower is these artists' chalet communities, little arcadian settlements that date back to the 1930s. Holtsfield became briefly notorious because a new landowner decided that he was best off without the thirty or so chalets and their residents, many of whom had been there for decades. A huge public battle erupted, with the residents garnering support from all corners.

I knew that the Holtsfield folk were likely to be pretty suspicious – and very understandably so – of any TV crew after their huge media exposure of a few years earlier. When Emyr and I went down there the week before to try and persuade them to let us film there and for a few of them to appear on camera having a chat with me, there wasn't much enthusiasm for the idea, but, after a very pleasant evening sat chatting around the great carved communal table outside, a few of them agreed to appear on camera.

It's shocking to think that such a settled, mature community that so obviously works brilliantly could be so easily threatened as it was between 1989 and 1997. And what a threat it was: the full force of the law, including bailiffs, summonses, evictions, the Court of Appeal and ultimately the House of Lords all employed against thirty or so people living quietly in a rustic corner of Gower. Holtsfield, and the other Gower communities like it, should be used in textbooks as prime examples of how to integrate people who live in close proximity to work as a healthy, happy and supportive unit. God knows, there are enough communities in the land at breaking point, where the first casualty has been any kind of trust between residents, and from that stems all manner of social, economic and even physical ills.

How successful Holtsfield has been can be seen by the length of time that many of its residents have lived there. Dai's been there for thirty years, and none of the other people around the table had managed anything less than twenty. Not that it's a middle-class hippy commune either. Most of the residents grew up in and around Swansea, and many work in the city in all kinds of jobs. Its success comes, said Dai, from this eclectic mixture of people and their values, which they've all got to learn to tolerate in order to be able to live together. I was very glad to have had the chance to see the place and meet some of its people. It was a real inspiration.

From the simple structures of Holtsfield back to the white leather banquettes of *Passage West*, we continued past some of southern Gower's best beaches. With the often strange-shaped limestone cliffs and lush vegetation, it was easy to imagine we were in Greece at times, rather than just a few miles from Swansea. One beach that regularly gets mentioned as Gower's finest rolled shortly into view. Three Cliffs Bay looked even better from the sea than it does from the land, and it looks absolutely magnificent from there. Again, this is one of those beaches – and there are loads on Gower – that benefits from being quite a way from any car park. There's at least a fifteen minute walk to get to Three Cliffs, and, because of that, it's never too busy. One of the best routes there is across Pennard Burrows, and through the sanded-over remains of Pennard Castle, sitting gloomily on the dunes and staring idly into space.

From here, it was one long sweep of sand past down to the curve of Oxwich Bay. Lying right beneath the bony ridge of Cefn Bryn, Oxwich is an old-fashioned kind of place which boasts, if that could be said to be the word, the only private beach on Gower. Most things hereabouts are in the ownership of the lords of Penrice Castle, just up the road, and it's only with his lordship's say so that we plebs are even allowed on the sands at all. Oxwich is kind of over-burdened, even by the ample standards of Wales, with castles. The Penrice estate contains two, the ruins of a thirteenth century fortress that you see along the main A4118, and a Georgian mansion to replace it, and, right above the beach, there's the Tudor fancy of Oxwich Castle, which also housed the same family for a while.

The end of Gower's one and only A-road comes in Port Eynon, the next bay after Oxwich Point. It's a busy and popular place, although there are major concerns that the beach is losing its sand because of offshore dredging. I hadn't been here for five or six years, and the extent of the loss stunned me. The village's old lifeboat station is now a superb YHA hostel with enviable views over the sinuous curve of Port Eynon Bay. It also overlooks the tumbledown remains of the old Salt House, once the centre of the district's extensive piracy and smuggling operations. In the seventeenth century, John Lucas of the Salt House was prosecuted for the "cozening of pirates and dangerous men". Sadly, they're all gone now.

I was keen to include in this programme somewhere that has just mesmerised since I first saw a photo of it, twenty-odd years ago. The

Culver Hole is a bricked-in cave, complete with four windows, in a narrow gash in the cliffs on the other side of the headland from the youth hostel. It's an eerie sight, and I can still recall the shiver that ran down my spine when I first saw that photo in a book about Wales. It looked so mysterious, aloof and even a little bit dangerous. I resolved to visit, although it wasn't until my second trip to Port Eynon that I finally found it, as the air of mystery and danger extends as far as the route you need to take to find it. Emyr, Dafydd and I, hacking over the headland with all the equipment, nearly got lost again this time, and this was my third visit. I don't suppose I'll find it any easier next time. It's a bit of a handicap, being a travel writer with a hopeless sense of direction.

With its dozens of standing stones, ancient forts, cairns and caves, there's a real air of mystery about much of Gower. But Culver Hole is definitely the greatest Gower enigma of them all. A sixty-foot wall, complete with windows, was wedged into the cleft of rock, and we still don't when or why. Was it an extension to long-gone Port Eynon Castle? A rich man's secret stronghold? A smuggling den? A pigeon loft? To some, our complete lack of certainty about this wonderfully spooky spot is a source of frustration, and efforts to prove its age and usage have

Emyr hauling the camera into the Culver Hole on a tow rope.

Deep inside the Culver Hole.

gone on for centuries. To me, it doesn't matter. If anything, the uncertainty only heightens the sense of awe that the Culver Hole generates. It exists, it's amazing, and that's good enough for me.

Filming the Culver Hole – once we'd finally found it – was a right palava. To gain access to the interior of the cave, you have to grapple up a rope to lift yourself fifteen feet up the rock face before making a very undignified hands-and-knees scramble across the threshold. Emyr, of course, wanted to film me doing just that, and it took a couple of goes to cover all the angles that he wanted. Then we had the even trickier task of getting him, Dafydd, and all of the equipment up inside so that I could finish my piece to camera about the place from deep within it. With an ingenious use of a car tow rope and a great deal of sweat, we managed it, and it was definitely worth the effort as the finished result looks commendably ghostly.

Travelling around the coast on the boat helped contextualise the Culver Hole for me, as we gained a clear view of it as we sailed past. It surely can't have been designed as anything very secretive, as all it would take to discover it is half-decent eyesight. The mystery deepens.

From here, it was a straight run along Gower's south-western coast to the flourish that is Worms Head, Pen Pyrod. This was a truly phenomenal section of coast, one that, even on its own, would have made the whole journey worthwhile, for you'll never get to see it any other way than on a boat. Improbably shaped limestone cliffs hundreds of feet high, hanging valleys that plunged through the rock like knives through butter and oodles of dark, dank caves drifted past us. It was stark, uncompromising and utterly stunning. Most famous of all the caves down here is Paviland, where, in 1823, a headless, red-stained skeleton was found and promptly christened the Red Lady of Paviland. The enormity of the discovery was unknown for the best part of a century, and it's only more recent techniques, especially radiocarbon dating, that have established it as hailing from around 22,000BC. And it also proved to be the skeleton of a man. Also in the cave were found more than eight hundred tools and implements.

My focus was firmly on Worms Head, looming large and exciting ahead of us. This is Gower's *pièce-de-resistance*, a swaggering geological exclamation mark at the end of the peninsula that snakes out for well over a mile from the bottom of Rhosili Bay. At high tide, it becomes an island, and numerous people are caught out there every year. I asked the lady in the National Trust shop at Rhosili how often it happens. "Oh, all the time," she replied. Well, what do you do? I asked. She pulled a bit of a face. "Depends who they are," was her deadpan reply.

Locally, Worms Head is known simply as The Worm. The name comes, as do so many south Gower names, from the Old English, in this case the word "wurm", which means dragon. The thinking there is that, in certain lights and from certain positions, the Worm takes on the appearance of a basking dragon. Sunset is one of the best times to appreciate the phenomenon, and it really works. Even the most flint-hearted of sceptics would begin to get a little bit mystical watching a flaming Rhosili sunset over the Worm.

Going around the headland on a boat was more exciting than I can possibly say. There's a famous blow-hole right at the tip, and, as we passed, we could hear the deep boom and splash as water funnelled at great speed up through the rock. Savage rock formations, a natural arch, crashing waves and a deep blue sea all combined in a riot of nature's finest pageantry. But this was as far as we could go on the *Passage West*, and, after taking it all in, Bob zapped the speed up and we dashed back to Swansea and the plastic charms of the Marina.

The next section of coast had to be done on foot, but that was no hardship, for it was Rhosili Bay, that glorious four-mile arc of perfect

The final flourish of Gower: Worms Head from the boat.

beach. Backed by the stark ridge of Rhosili Down, and tucked in between the high water islets of Worms Head and Burry Holms, Rhosili Bay brings out the five-year-old in anyone. It makes you want to sing and swoop, fly kites, run into the sea holding hands with your auntie, dig sandcastles and wait for your freckles to break out.

Almost exactly half-way along the sands is a beautiful white Georgian house. This is the Old Rectory, and it's way out on its own not because vicars are innately anti-social, but because the priest of Rhosili also had to cover the parish of Llangennith at the other end of Rhosili Bay, so positioning the rectory mid-way between the two made sense. These days, the Old Rectory is a National Trust holiday home – in fact, *the* most popular of all their rentable properties. It's booked up for peak season years in advance. All the more bizarre, therefore, that, when the Wales Tourist Board brought out a brochure that included a large photo of the bay, someone had seen fit to airbrush the Old Rectory from it. Does a handsome Georgian rectory, snuggled in a perfect position, not fit in with the WTB's vision of the country they are given millions of pounds of taxpayers' money to promote? I can't help but think that, had there been a golf course there instead, they'd have left that alone.

North of Rhosili is another splendid sandy beach, Broughton Bay, which stares out at Carmarthenshire across the water. Here, we hooked up with British kite-surfing champion Kirsty Jones, who was charged with the almost impossible task of getting me kite-surfing in a couple of hours. It's one of the newest adrenaline water sports around, and Kirsty, a Pembrokeshire lass, has proved to be its greatest exponent so far. In 2002, she kite-surfed all the way from Ireland to Wales in just five hours, and last year, crossed the English Channel the same way.

First, she got me flying one of her power-kites on land. Having only ever ponced around with a kite on a Sunday afternoon in the park, this beast of a kite was a different animal altogether. Once the wind took it, it was impossible to stay still, and I found myself being pulled across the sands at speeds I haven't managed for years, the sockets of my shoulders straining like a mad dog on a lead. Kirsty decided that I was then ready for the next challenge, to be "body-dragged" across the water by the kite. It was amazing, even when I fell over in less than a foot of water and was dragged along at high speed by the kite, my knees virtually scraping the bottom as I shot through the waves. She was great, and my memories of that afternoon still rate as one of the hilarious highlights of the trip.

There was no way our ostentatious cabin cruiser could cope with the final section of the journey, along the north side of Gower. This is the very shallow estuary of Afon Llwchwr, or River Loughor, so we called on

Kitesurfing is perhaps not one of my career options

Gwyn and Phil from the Loughor Boat Club to escort us up to Penclawdd. Northern Gower is such a different landscape to the south of the peninsula. Gone are the dramas in limestone, to be replaced by marshland, mudflats, shifting sandbanks, grazing wild ponies and a gentle green coastline punctuated by snug little villages, such as Llanmadoc, Landimore and Llanrhidian.

All the differences between the two halves of Gower are down to geology. Like Pembrokeshire, there's a north-south split, culturally, economically and linguistically. The limestone south and west of Gower were the most attractive and fertile lands for invaders to grab, which they did with efficient gusto. Viking and then Norman settlers in these parts ensured that the native Welsh barely got a look-in, and explains the English-sounding names all along its shores. The northern and eastern of Gower, however, is more shale and coal deposits, which proved to be of no real interest to invaders, so the Welsh were allowed that part. Same old story. Even today, villages like Crofty, Llanmorlais and Penclawdd look, feel and sound much, much more Welsh than anywhere else on Gower. Penclawdd, of course, is synonymous with the cockle industry, although, when we were there in the summer of 2003, cockling was still banned due to impurities found in the regular tests that are conducted. Controversy still rages about the efficacy of these tests, and it's to be hoped that this most traditional of industries can yet be saved.

For the end of the programme, we returned almost to the place where we started, high up on Cefn Bryn and overlooking the entire peninsula. We shot the final sequence up at sunset, by the legendary King Arthur's Stone, the Maen Ceti, a vast and imperious monolith that completely blew me away when I first saw it. Its siting, so effortlessly commanding, made me think that this was the Guv'nor of Gower, the place to which the whole peninsula had angled itself for four and a half thousand years. More than any other journey in *Coast to Coast*, I felt as if I'd spent a week in a foreign country while we'd been on Gower. It's not really Wales, it's certainly not England, it's just Gower. A place apart, a nearly-island.

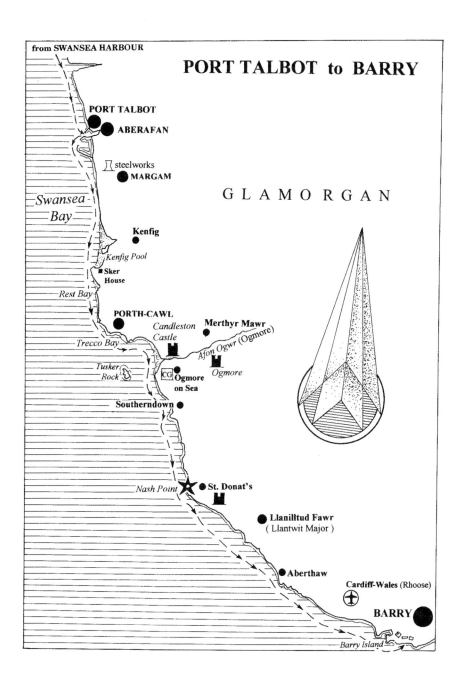

from SWANSEA HARBOUR

PORT TALBOT to BARRY

PORT TALBOT

ABERAFAN

steelworks

MARGAM

Swansea Bay

G L A M O R G A N

Kenfig

Kenfig Pool

■ **Sker House**

Rest Bay

PORTH-CAWL

Candleston Castle

Merthyr Mawr

Trecco Bay

Afon Ogwr (Ogmore)

Tusker Rock

CG **Ogmore on Sea**

Ogmore

Southerndown

Nash Point ★ ● **St. Donat's**

Llanilltud Fawr
(Llantwit Major)

● **Aberthaw**

Cardiff-Wales (Rhoose)

BARRY

Barry Island

CHAPTER ELEVEN:

PORT TALBOT - BARRY

Hiya Byt!

Almost a journey between the country's two main cities, this populous coastline should, in theory, be the most heavily exploited in Wales. But nature has taken its own path and has seen fit to render much of the coast inhabitable and inhospitable. It makes for some dramatic contrasts: where the terrain allows, outposts of the Valleys pour through to spread along as much coast as physically possible. Planes buzzing overhead to Cardiff Airport and tankers rolling by remind you constantly that you're far from the middle of nowhere. And yet, in between the planes and boats and Barratt estates, the sense of isolation and wilderness is so strong that it's intoxicating.

This was the first programme that we filmed in the second series. I was a tiny bit nervous as to how I'd feel getting back on a boat after such a disastrous final day on Llŷn the previous year. The experience had knocked me right out of kilter for a month or so afterwards – all of my friends could see it and were pretty worried for a bit. I was physically very ill for a week or so, and then emotionally flat on the floor for weeks. It had been much the same for Dafydd and Emyr, who had shared that awful journey. I hadn't even wanted to go near the sea for a while after that, and I certainly hadn't been on a boat since. So, as I drove into Swansea Harbour, looking for Port Talbot Diving and Marine, there were a few little butterflies skittering around inside.

The fear only finally vanished when I set foot on the *Strathdoon*, Port

Talbot Marine's working vessel, an old industrial tug. The smell of rust, diesel and seawater hit my nostrils and all I felt was excitement about going out to sea for six more journeys and six more indulgent looks at Wales from the water. I couldn't wait.

The Strathdoon, our vessel for the voyage.

And it was great to be re-united with the team. More than anything else (save for the coast itself), it was the teamwork with such talented colleagues that really made *Coast to Coast* for me. Having been self-employed as a writer for twelve years now, I was eager to get stuck in to some work that was more co-operative, that depended on the skill and ingenuity of others, just as much as it depended on mine. I was also getting a bit fed up with words, and their limitations, a situation that hadn't really been helped by my few years playing at being a stand-up comedian – again, very solitary and all words, words, words. The urge to work on something more visual had been growing for a couple of years. When, at the very last minute, HTV (sorry, ITV1 Wales) had commissioned me to do a one-off "my take on Wales" half-hour programme for St David's Day in 2002 (*The Dragon's Trail* – they wouldn't let me get away with *Chasing the Dragon*), it was pure luck that they teamed me up with Emyr Jenkins. We worked together on that, racing round Wales in February and clicked immediately, so I was delighted when he was asked to work on the series a few months later. He has an amazing sense of a programme as a huge jigsaw, and his ability to work out all the pieces and how to get them is phenomenal. Not only that, we shared a lot of similar opinions and outlooks, as well as taste in dodgy jokes and even dodgier bars. His genius filming, teasing the absolute best out of the views we were seeing, was such a major part of the appeal of *Coast to Coast*. The vast majority of it was done with just one camera – Emyr's, and how he managed to make something so necessarily cheap look so damn classy will always amaze me.

With the exception of changing Dafydds – Dafydd Parry in the first series, Dafydd Baines in the second – on sound, the *Coast to Coast* team remained the same for both series. Emyr and I were half of it, Helen Williams-Ellis, the ebullient originator of the idea and Series Producer, and Guto Williams, researcher and laconic fall guy for anything that went wrong, were the other half. I like to think that we became quite a well-oiled little machine by the end of it – regularly well-oiled, if the truth be told.

The image that came to mind when I was thinking about this journey was a sandwich. The bread on either side is pure white sliced Mother's Pride; plain and simple, in the shape of two ports purpose built for the coal trade of the Valleys, namely Port Talbot and Barry. The filling of the sandwich is a far posher affair, in the cliffs and coves of the wealthy Vale of Glamorgan, that saggy, satisfied jowl at the bottom of the map of Wales.

To most of us, Port Talbot is just a blur of grey rooves and belching steelworks as we zoom through on the M4. Few people except the locals know that it has a superb, broad, long beach, although technically, the beach is in Aberafan (Aberavon), Port Talbot's Siamese twin. Even more confusingly, what you see today is the third Aberafan – the previous two were swallowed by the waters of the ever-expanding Bristol Channel. Whose to say it couldn't happen again? The residents of the Sandfields estate, tucked behind the shore and its half-hearted seaside trappings, had better keep a look out.

We chugged out of Swansea, though in order to pretend that we were leaving Port Talbot, we had to nip up the estuary of Afon Afan towards the town's docks. We couldn't land, as that would have cost us six hundred quid to the port authority, so the crew – Steve, Tony and Ross – got us in, turned us round and got us out again without so much as touching a barnacle. Steve, our skipper, pointed out the piers and buttresses that they had refurbished at Port Talbot from this very boat.

The Port Talbot (Margam)
steelworks from the sea

140

Port Talbot Diving and Marine are local maritime troubleshooters, able at a moment's notice to build, repair and assist on both sea and shore. It's an old family company dating back forty years – indeed, Ross, one of our crew, is the company founder's grandson, and his dad still puts in some time.

From the sea, Port Talbot and Aberafan were dwarfed by the humungous Corus steelworks spread along the shore for a well over a mile. It is claimed that the night-time view of the steelworks, together with the chemical works at Baglan, inspired Ridley Scott with the idea for the futuristic city in *Bladerunner*. There is some fantastical element to the sight of them, even more so when you see that they are placed slap next to beautiful sandy beaches.

Behind the steelworks, we could just make out the gothic turrets of Margam Castle at the heart of its Country Park. Although gutted by fire in 1977, from which it's never fully recovered, Margam still gives off an air of haughty indulgence – not surprising, perhaps, when you consider that it was designed and built in the 1830s by Thomas Hopper, also responsible for the vulgar ostentation of Penrhyn Castle at Bangor. Margam was built for Victorian entrepreneur Christopher Talbot (of Port Talbot), infamous as the quietest MP of all time. Despite representing Glamorgan in Westminster for some fifty-nine years, it is said that he only ever made one contribution to debate, and that was to ask someone to close the window as he was sitting in a draught.

Margam Moors, running down to the sea, merge pretty seamlessly with the vast dune system that has engulfed the medieval port of Kenfig, once Glamorgan's third largest borough, after Cardiff and Swansea. Nowadays, the M4 tears through the dunes at its eastern end, but somehow the highway-on-stilts echoing to the whoosh of traffic only adds to the sense of other-worldliness about the place. The town, which was established in the Bronze Age, fought many battles against the encroaching sands, but, as ever, nature won out and the whole town – church, houses, streets and castle – finally disappeared almost overnight in the sixteenth century in a huge sandstorm. We filmed at the only visible remnant, the top of the fifty-foot castle keep that pokes its wrecked head out of the sands. Wales has more castles per mile than any other country in Europe – around six hundred. Kenfig has to be just about the weirdest of them all. The site, surrounded by miles of gloomy dune and with the M4 and mainline railway hurtling past, is spectacularly melancholy.

Not surprisingly, the lost town has spawned its fair share of ghost tales. Most famous is the ghost of Kenfig's *Prince of Wales* pub, built in the sixteenth century as the new town hall to replace the one that had disappeared under the sands. The *Prince of Wales* is a cracking pub – a warren of little rooms, shiny woodwork, polished brass and fine beer drawn by hand. We ended up having lunch here on numerous occasions, as Emyr and I both became hopelessly addicted to their bargain bowls of faggots and peas.

The pub's gaffer, Richard Ellis, told me about his celebrated ghost. I've got to say that I'm always a bit suspicious of pub ghosts, which often seem to be little more than canny marketing techniques for gullible tourists. But the documentary and anecdotal evidence at Kenfig is pretty strong. Richard confessed that he'd always been sceptical too and, although he'd never actually seen a ghost, he'd experienced numerous strange and irrational sensations in the place. He lent us a tape that we used in the programme, which was of the sounds recorded in the pub walls some twenty years ago. Under strict scientific conditions, electrodes were placed in the wall, and attached to a bank of tape recorders which were left running all night. They were found to contain the sound of voices conversing in Old Welsh, organ music and a ticking clock, although there was no clock in the place at the time.

There are more phantoms just down the road at the magnificently atmospheric Sker House. An Elizabethan manor sat aloof and alone in the fields above the sea, Sker was a crumbling ruin until a few years back, when it was taken over by the Buildings at Risk Trust (BART), a charity set up to rescue historic houses from ruin, before selling them on. By a happy coincidence, when Emyr and I were recceing the area prior to the filming, we were tucking into our customary faggots at the *Prince of Wales* when we happened to get talking with Alan Bemrose, Chairman of BART who had come down for the day for a site visit to Sker. We persuaded him to let us go and have a look with him.

It was fantastic. The house just takes your breath away, with its stone-flagged rooms and winding staircases, vast wooden beams and grand main hall, complete with eighteenth century graffiti on one of its walls. I'd seen a BBC film of Sker from a couple of years earlier, when the house was little more than a gaunt ruin. The creaks and groans of the structure were evidently terrifying the crew, and, when they made their way up to the attic room where the Maid of Sker, whose name became a famous novel by R. D. Blackmore, author of *Lorna Doone*, had been imprisoned, things became very hairy. The Maid, the daughter of the house, was locked in her garret for the simple crime of falling in love with the wrong man and her miserable ghost is said to haunt the room still. Just as the BBC crew, led by a ghostbuster who'd bustled her way up to the Maid's room without a moment's hesitation, arrived, a huge crash was heard downstairs. The crew fled, the lighting man dropping the light, which promptly exploded.

When we took the crew to Sker (for a sequence that sadly had to be omitted from the final programme, due to time restrictions), nothing so terrifying happened to us. In fact, the work that BART have undertaken on the house seems to have exorcised it of its demons. The atmosphere when we were there, with the renovations nearing completion and the house about to be placed on the market for nearly £1 million, was undeniably benign and even welcoming. For all the prophecies of doom that have swirled around Sker for decades, it seemed that the old house had responded well to some serious TLC. Hearing about BART was fascinating – they have saved hundreds of at-risk buildings all over the UK and operate on an absolute shoestring.

Sker House, now painted a warm primrose yellow, looked deeply impressive from the water as we clunked our way past. It's an astonishing spot, if only because it feels so very remote when you're there, but from the sea its close proximity to Porthcawl was glaring. The approach to this famous seaside resort from the west is dominated, rather appropriately, by the Royal Porthcawl Golf Club, and we could see dozens of ageing gents spread over its greens. The beach in front of the golf course is Rest Bay, one of the most celebrated in south Wales for surfing, and there were plenty there when we passed by. It's a funny old mix, golfers and surfers, but it works happily enough, though I doubt that there's much of an overlap between the two groups.

Around the headland, and we got a good full frontal of Porthcawl itself. Founded as a Victorian port that never really took off, it was the coming of the cult of the seaside that made the town, and it quickly became one of the main resorts for the tens of thousands of people who would pour down from the pits and terraces of the Valleys. Although the same can be said of all seaside resorts, its heyday has long passed, but you get the feeling that Porthcawl hasn't quite worked out how to play it from here. That said, with the popularity of Rest Bay as the nearest surf beach for folk from Cardiff, together with a catchment area of a million people, Porthcawl should find its way through.

There's certainly a stronger air of confidence in the town than when I first visited, on *Rough Guide* duty, a decade ago. I'm ashamed to say that, in that first edition, I gave the town an absolute drubbing, and not really for any valid reasons. Sure, the place looked a bit clapped-out (but then, so did just about every other seaside resort), but it was the fact that the woman in the tourist office was so unpleasant to me that made me decide to have my very unprofessional revenge by rubbishing both her office and the town as a whole. I blush at the memory.

I can't deny that such irrational prejudice has occasionally shaped the writing of the *Rough Guide to Wales*. Especially for the first edition, when I was often seeing places for the first time, any small irrelevance could blow the whole account apart. It might be raining and/or half-day closing. You might get cut up for a parking space. Someone gives you some gyp in a shop. You tread in some dog shit. Or you're just in a foul mood and nothing, but nothing, is going to be allowed to shift it. For any or all of these reasons, it's just too easy to haughtily dismiss somewhere as ugly, boring, unfriendly or whatever. As the years have rolled by, and new editions have been written, the really unfair examples of bias have been ironed out, if only because repeated visits have meant more rounded experiences, and accounts, of places, and, I'd like to think, a little bit of maturing on the part of the authors.

Also indicating that Porthcawl may be on the up-and-up is the refurbished Grand Pavilion, which, from the sea, lords it over the rest of the Promenade with considerable chutzpah. This was where the great Miners' Galas were held, occasions brimming over with passion and purpose. Paul Robeson, the black American singer and civil rights activist who became a great admirer and friend of the miners of south Wales, was due to address one such gala in the early 1950s, but was banned from leaving the USA, at the height of the McCarthy era of witch-hunts against commies and pinkos. Instead, a phone line was sorted out which was rigged up to a PA system in the Grand Pavilion, and thousands of miners listened to Robeson's baritone exhortations for better conditions for the working classes, in America, Wales and the world. It's hard to imagine such febrile, urgent politics taking place there now, amongst the bingo sessions and gigs by 1960s has-beens.

Perhaps the most dramatic sight Porthcawl has to offer from the sea is the huge caravan park at Trecco Bay, said to be the largest in Europe. There are whole communities from the Valleys who have re-located to Trecco Bay, and who now replicate the close-knit housing of their home towns in their caravans and chalets. It's an echo of the earlier miners' shanty-towns that would erupt every summer on the dunes of Trecco and Kenfig. In the early decades of the twentieth century, entire communities would jalopy their way down to the dunes, household furniture precariously balanced on carts, and set up tent cities in the sands. Reports tell of impromptu holiday camps breaking out, with hundreds of people in tents and under tarpaulins, catching and cooking rabbits, making music and singing and dancing round huge fires, galloping over the beaches and splashing around in the sea. It sounds wonderful.

144

The chocolate box charms of Merthyr Mawr village

From the so-called biggest caravan park in Europe, it was just a short hop to the largest sand dune in Europe, at Merthyr Mawr. Unlike the dune system at Kenfig, most of which is now grown over by grass and greenery, Merthyr Mawr is still satisfyingly dune-like, with its acres of fine orange sand. No surprise, therefore, that it doubled up as the Middle East in some of the scenes in the 1960s blockbuster version of *Lawrence of Arabia*. It's only five miles from Kenfig, but it feels like five hundred. The dune's inland edge is lush and almost tropical, as opposed to the light industry of Kenfig. Deep within the exuberant greenery at Merthyr Mawr are the hush-hush ruins of Candeleston Castle, a fifteenth-century manor house cloaked in ivy, and a far remove from the scratchy stumps of Kenfig Castle by the M4. But the starkest difference between the two dune systems comes when you go inland just a few hundred yards more. From Kenfig, you're swiftly into the functional Valleys housing of Pyle. At Merthyr Mawr, you meander into the village of the same name, which looks more like it's sprung from the pages of Thomas Hardy, with its thatched cottages, groaning orchards and village green. Hard to believe that you're only a mile or two from the middle of Bridgend.

Zzzzzzzz on the village green at Merthyr Mawr

On yet another visit to the *Prince of Wales* at Kenfig, some of the regulars told us to go down to the Dipping Bridge at Merthyr Mawr. Its name comes from the days when farmers would dip their sheep in the Afon Ogwr, by pushing them through holes in the bridge. Nowadays, it's just the local kids and teenagers who dip themselves in the river, as there's a deep pool just downstream that they can hurtle themselves into from the bridge's parapet. Even the oldest of the old boys in the pub reminisced happily about doing this in his youth, and it's a practise that continues today. We made our way down to the bridge, and, late on a baking hot summer's afternoon, found it humming with life. There were dozens of lads and lasses just hanging out there, swimming in the river, somersaulting off the bridge, having a great time. It was fantastic to see.

This spot, so spontaneously joyous on a summer's day, has a murkier secret, for this was also the site of operation for one of the most notorious serial killers in Welsh history. The lane that crosses the bridge is an old Roman way, the Via Julia Maritima, and was, for many centuries, the main pilgrim route from Llandaff and southern Wales to St David's. By the bridge used to be a pub, the New Inn, whose nineteenth century landlord had something of a penchant for robbing and bumping off pilgrims as they came to seek refreshment. When the site was excavated in the early twentieth century, dozens of human remains were found in the garden and the field opposite where the pub had been.

The eastern boundary of the Merthyr Mawr warren is the estuary of Afon Ogwr, the river Ogmore, where the landscape changed immediately. Gone were the rolling dunes, to be replaced by the pale yellow triassic cliffs so redolent of the Vale coastline. It's absolutely unique in Wales. The perfect geometry of the limestone and shale layers, punched by occasional caves, is a glorious sight, and we were getting it at its perfect best from the boat on a clear, hot day. There are some superb beaches along this stretch too, from the open sweep of Dunraven Bay at Southerndown to the remote "clothing optional" coves near Monknash, all backed by the distinctive stratified cliffs.

The contours of the cliffs climbed as we approached the two lighthouses at Nash Point. To navigate the boat around the Point requires some precision, as there is a large sandbank lurking just below the water's surface all the way along this part of the coast. There are a fair few hereabouts in fact, including Tusker Rock off Ogmore and a large bank off Porthcawl that has been the subject of plans for an offshore wind farm. Surprisingly, Nash Point was the last lighthouse in Wales to remain manned. The last lighthouse keeper left as it was switched to full automation as recently as 2000.

Rounding Nash Point, we quickly came to the little quay below St Donat's Castle, now the international Atlantic College. There's something very make-believe about St Donat's: from the sea, it looked more like a two-dimensional film set that a good heave-ho would easily flatten. Perhaps it's a subconscious nod to the castle's most important date with destiny, when it was bought in the 1925 by American press magnate William Randolph Hearst, famously the character on whom Orson Welles based his portrayal in *Citizen Kane*. He had a Welsh mistress and was looking for a suitable pile in which to install her – makes a nice change from the back of a Vauxhall Vectra, I suppose. Hearst spent a fortune doing up the dowdy neo-Gothic heap, including bumping up the number of bathrooms from Welsh standards (three) to American standards (nearly forty).

The awesome Vale of Glamorgan coast near Llantwit Major

Just a couple of miles further on, with the cliffs still tall, proud and very dramatic, we came to the little slash in the landscape where Afon Col-Huw disgorges itself into the Bristol Channel. This is the beach to the nearby town of Llanilltud Fawr, or Llantwit Major, and is a place I regularly visit when I'm staying with mates in Cardiff for a breath of sea air and a good dog walk. There's just a car park, a beach strewn with vast limestone boulders and a small caff there, and it's a perfect combination. One time I was there supping a post-walk cuppa outside the cafe when a group of three or four lads ambled over to me. "Scuse me mate," one said. "You don't happen to know what that island over there is do you?", he asked as he gestured expansively across the channel. "Island? Over there?" I replied, straining hard to see anything against the ever-present backdrop of Somerset. "Yeah, that one," replied the lad, his arm sweeping across the whole cross-channel landscape. "That's Somerset," I said. Blank faces all round. "That's England." England becomes an offshore island of Wales – now there's a turn-up for the books.

Welsh place-names – often evocative and with a real poetry of their own – don't always survive anglicisation very well. Dinbych-y-pysgod – the little fort of the fishes – sounds so dull as Tenby, though that's nothing compared with the indignity suffered for years by Abaty Cwm Hir – the abbey of the long valley – which the Victorians managed to mangle into Come Here Abbey. But the plumpest turkey of them all is Llanilltud Fawr, the great llan of St Illtud, which somehow managed to emerge as Llantwit Major. That'd really draw the crowds wouldn't it? "Come and hear the great St Twit preach!" Mind you, there's a fair few men of the cloth, past and present, who'd fit that particular title.

Llantwit is perhaps the best example of a phenomenon that never ceases to amaze me about Wales. At school in Worcestershire, just forty miles from the border, British history taught me that the period between when the Romans left in the fifth century and the Norman invasion of 1066 was the Dark Ages, a time when the country plunged back into barbaric tribalism and illiterate grunts. Well, that may have been the case in England, but it certainly wasn't so in Wales. The so-called Dark Ages were, in fact, something of a Golden Age here, when trade and learning were paramount, and men of faith were educated in the highest disciplines. The monastery at Llanilltud Fawr was one of the educational powerhouses of the age, attracting students as eminent as St David and St Patrick. Some of the ruins are clustered around the sumptuous parish church of St Illtud, really two churches in one, and a place that I always find to be a real haven of peace, especially compared with the rest of this bustling little town with its improbably narrow streets.

The last segment of coast, although still predominantly limestone cliffs and sandy beaches, takes on an altogether more industrial look to it as it nears Barry and Cardiff. Towering units, power lines and planes all increased as we neared the clean-cut shape of Aberthaw power station, dazzling white against the deep blue sky. It's something of a dying breed, in that it's the last power station in Wales to be powered by Welsh coal, namely the stuff brought down from Tower Colliery, the last deep mine in the Valleys.

We were soon humming past the straggled village of Rhoose. Behind the village, jumbo jets could be seen sat on the tarmac of Cardiff-Wales Airport, and there were constant planes buzzing overhead. So much more the surprise, therefore, when I spotted a cliff-top caravan park right at the end of the airport's main runway. Who the hell would want a holiday there? Planespotters? Looking on the map, I see that between the runway and the caravan park is the Vale of Glamorgan railway that is due to be brought back into passenger service by 2005, so at least they'll be able to get a bit of trainspotting in as well. Blimey, I bet a night in the bar down there would feel like a lifetime.

If poor St Illtud saw his town corrupted to Llantwit, old St Baruch didn't fare much better. His little village became the town of Barry, who sounds as if he should be the patron saint of white socks and souped-up GTIs. As a town, Barry is only a little more than a century old, having developed as a great rival coal port to Cardiff. Not only was it a mighty port in its heyday, it also developed as a cheap'n'cheerful seaside resort, mostly focussed on the knobble of land known as Barry Island.

The factory fortnight at Barry Island may be long gone, but it's still a decent place for a good seaside blowout. One of my editors at *Big Issue Cymru*, Cathryn Scott, is a Barry girl, and I hooked up with her for a go on a few of the Barry Island rides. We decided to try and do the interview on the pirate ship, that huge semi-circular swing that whooshes nauseously from side to side. Emyr and Dafydd sat in the middle of the ship, camera pointing up towards Cath and I sat a few rows further up. There was a young lad bouncing around, very keen to be filmed, so Emyr got him sat just behind us, and made him promise not to look at the camera. He was as good as his word, and off we went for a good ten minutes, Cath and I chatting happily, Emyr and Dafydd getting it all recorded. Once the pirate ship had stopped, Emyr and Dafydd got off so that they could film us from the ground and intercut the images. The young lad behind us started to get off. Emyr ran up to him – "don't you want another go?" "No thanks," the lad replied. "Well, you'll have to," Emyr insisted, "otherwise the continuity will be all messed up. One minute you'll be in the shots, the next not. Go on, just one more go."

So off we all went again, the lad slumped behind us and looking none too happy about the prospect. This time, because the camera and sound

Cathryn Scott and I (and the poor little vomit monster behind) on the Pirate Ship at Barry Island.

equipment were now all off the pirate ship, we were able to go higher and the operator took great delight in pushing us up as far as we could go. Cath and I were getting a little hysterical when we suddenly both heard a strange heaving sound and smelt a foul reek. I turned round to see the poor lad behind us sitting in the largest pool of vomit I have ever seen, his face as green as a sprout as he slid up and down the plastic bench in a sea of bile and diced carrots. He was covered in it, and stank. Cathryn and I both tried shouting down to the operator to slow down, get us back to earth, but he either didn't hear or didn't care. We were going for another five minutes, during which time the lad somehow managed to find yet more undigested lunch to honk all over his seat. Eventually, we were let back down to the ground, and, as the poor little lad staggered off, he was confronted by a grinning Emyr in blissful ignorance. "Thanks a lot for that," he said, digging into his pocket. "Here's a quid. Go get yourself an ice cream."

Caption (pic Dewi Glyn Jones)

Even Barry, that quintessence of the *Hi-de-Hi!* world of knobbly knees contests and glamorous grannies, is changing. We wandered over to the old Butlin's camp, where security guards patrol the padlocked gates and the chalets have been demolished to make way for fussy Executive Homes with state-of-the-art security systems. Down at the Knap, the town's biggest bay, the glorious old lido pool moulders away behind barbed wire fences, while stylish new apartments (with names like Sydney and Malibu) spring up on the shore. But there were plenty of people around, the arcades were busy, cafes and pubs full and the donkeys were shuffling up and down the beaches. It was good to see that, while the British love affair with the seaside may have adapted and changed over the years, it's still there and I really don't think it'll ever die.

P.S. More eagle-eyed readers will spot a small gap in the Welsh coast between Barry, the end of this journey, and Newport, the end of the next one. It's a small gap indeed, but it does happen to contain Cardiff, our beloved capital city. In the twelve episodes of *Coast to Coast*, we had to make tough choices about leaving some places out, and I'm rather proud of the fact that Cardiff fell into that category. Our reasoning was simple enough. Any TV viewer in Wales will already be so familiar with the capital city, thanks to its endless promotion on screen, that there was little we could usefully add.

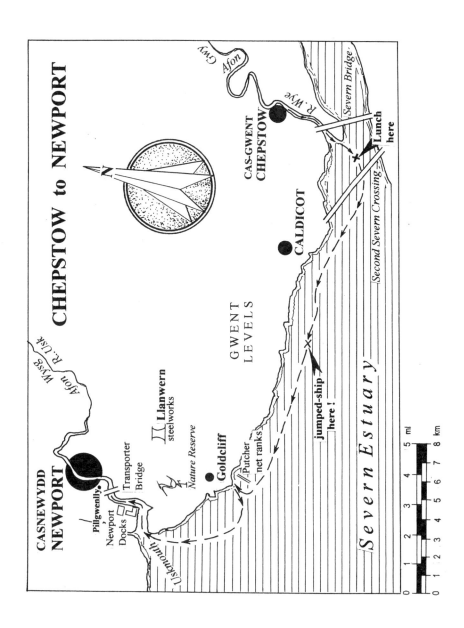

CHEPSTOW to NEWPORT

CHAPTER TWELVE:
CHEPSTOW - NEWPORT
That Sinking Feeling

One of the things that makes working for television so exciting is how easy it is sometimes to make things happen. I get a bit hacked off with TV's reverential self-importance, but there's no denying how effective it is as a medium and how helpful people normally are for a telly crew. When we were planning the first series, Emyr, Helen, Guto and I sat around in the Caernarfon offices of Cwmni Da, mulling over possible routes and the boats to take us on them. When a chug down the Severn Estuary was proposed, my first thought was "let's get something like a dredger." Three or four weeks later, there we were, filming aboard said dredger. Easy.

This was by far the biggest craft we ever encountered during *Coast to Coast*. The dredger *Brackland* is over four hundred tons empty, and more than twice that when it's full. It's part of the flotilla of Fred Larkham, one of Monmouthshire's most legendary characters. Everywhere we went during the filming, when we mentioned that we were sailing with Fred, eyebrows would shoot up and chuckles erupt, for Fred's fleet is infamous hereabouts. He collects boats on their way to the knacker's yard, and has about half a dozen of them stacked alongside the shore at Chepstow, slap on the Wales-England border.

We became intimately acquainted with all of Fred's boats when we had to climb over them, one by one, to reach the *Brackland*. As the Severn tidal basin (which includes the River Wye at Chepstow) has the second highest drop of any tide in the world, you can only set sail at precisely the right stage in the tide, roughly a third of the way between high and low. At high tide, Fred re-positioned the *Brackland* off the shore side and into the mid-channel of the river, securing it there as the tide began to drop. An hour or so later, we had to board, and the only way to do so was to leapfrog our way over the four or five rusting hulks between the dredger and the shore. This required climbing ladders, jumping from one deck to another, scrambling up ship sides and more nimble dexterity than I'd been called on to display since the days of school PE lessons. As if that wasn't enough of a challenge, Emyr, Dafydd and I had to do it carrying stacks of camera and sound equipment.

To turn the boat round and head downstream, Fred basically has to let the powerful falling tide do the work. Once we were all aboard, he fired up the engine, raised the anchor pole from the river bed and the boat started to turn. It's an exhilaratingly close thing, as the boat swung round, missing the cliffs on the English side of the river by a matter of just a few feet. We were on our way. Quite honestly, I've never been that fussed about Chepstow, a town that seems to have squandered its best assets quite shamefully. A great castle but little else. So it was no hardship to be getting out of town pretty sharpish. And boy, what a getaway vehicle.

At Chepstow alone, the normal range between high and low tide is some forty-nine feet. This awesomely powerful tide, second only to the Bay of Fundy on the USA-Canada border, would, not suprisingly, come to dominate the journey, and anyone who sails in the Severn Estuary has to be intimately aware of it.

The first leg of the journey, down the last few miles of the 135-mile long River Wye, or Afon Gwy, took us past wooded cliffs and few signs of human habitation. Looming large ahead of us was the old Severn Bridge, awaiting us around the final corner as the Wye disgorges itself into the Severn. The swirling brown water, lowering sky and mournful shrieks of the seabirds gave it a very melancholy atmosphere, and made me think of the poor suicidal souls for whom great bridges like this are but magnets. The old Severn Bridge, built in 1966 and instantly connecting south Wales and south-west England in a way that had never previously happened, became particularly notorious in February 1995, when the abandoned car of Richey Edwards, of the Manic Street Preachers, was found at Aust service station on the English side. Did he jump? Or do a runner? It's just one of the many mysteries that the bridge holds.

The new Severn Bridge, just a few miles downstream, looked wonderful as we glided with the tide down the estuary. "We'll stop here for lunch," Fred said, and, no sooner said than done, the piledriver anchor was lowered into the bed and we sat still. Fred's crew, a lad called Jason, had been busy cooking a roast chicken dinner, which we all tucked into with great enthusiasm in the *Brackland's* crew quarters down below deck. On the walls were pictures of the ship's launch back in the early 1960s. The gleaming new boat in the photos was pretty hard to square with the rusty hulk it had become over the decades. Lunch was wonderful, and I had to pinch myself that I was eating such fine food on a gorgeous summer's day in the middle of the River Severn mid-way between its two great road bridges. Both banks of the river are highly developed, and everywhere you look, man's busy little hand is evident. But out here, all was quiet and calm and even slightly eerie.

The dredger Brackland in the Severn estuary

The contrast was even more marked when we actually sailed under the magnificent new bridge and could see the traffic charging over it, like rows of busy ants, hell-bent on some distant destination, while we glided along at a stately pace with only the noise of seagulls for company. I've got to say that, while thundering across the Severn Bridge accompanied by some great music and good mates can undoubtedly be a lot of fun, there's absolutely no contest. I mean, whoever heard of estuary rage?

Steering through the channel under the new bridge is quite a challenge, for this is a mighty stretch of water. The bridge is built on a series of rocky outcrops, with the shipping channel in a gap of just one hundred feet between them. The gap is known as The Shoots, as this is exactly what you do when you sail through it. With the combined power of the huge tide and Wales' two biggest rivers funnelling through the opening, navigation is not for the inexperienced or faint hearted. Fred showed me the section on his maritime navigation chart. Even if you go through at an idling speed of just two knots, the power of the tidal surge will make you go at a pretty dynamic 14 or 15 knots. It was like being in a 400 ton kayak.

You will notice there that I call the River Severn, or Afon Hafren, a

What a sight – the new Severn Bridge from below

Welsh river, for so it is. Although the river, the longest on this island, meanders most of its course through what is, these days, administratively England, it is unquestionably Welsh, rising in the misty, boggy moorland of Pumlumon in mid Wales before snaking its way 220 miles through the borderlands to the sea. If Owain Glyndŵr had succeeded, this mellifluous waterway would have been the eastern boundary of his independent Wales, harking back to the earlier border of the ancient Kingdom of Powys.

Having grown up by the Severn in northern Worcestershire, it's long been a river that has fascinated me. It has so many moods. There's the gurgling, peaty stream pumping down off the hills, the bright and bubbling infant river flowing through Llanidloes and Newtown, the languid beast, prone to rising up and flooding, that I knew in the Bewdley, Stourport and Worcester of my childhood, and finally, the yawning chocolate-brown estuary as it flows out into the Bristol Channel. And it is definitely a natural border between England and Wales. Great Severnside boroughs like Shrewsbury, Worcester and Gloucester feel like frontier towns, places where two nations meet to trade and tipple, guzzle and gossip together.

Dredging began a couple of miles into the estuary. The calmness of the journey down river was shattered by the raging torrent of sandy water rapidly filling up the hold. It's a spectacular sight, as was the river slowly creeping up the side of the boat as we become heavier and heavier. The *Brackland* holds about 450 tons of sand, plus about 100 tons of water, and, after a couple of hours it's absolutely full. The water pouring off the hold was everywhere, rushing over the deck, spilling out of every rusty hole going.

After two hours, with the hold full, Fred and Jason were due to turn around and chug their ponderous way back up to Chepstow. Our journey was to continue courtesy of another boat in Fred's fleet, namely an ex-landing craft that saw service in the Falklands War, skippered by his son. We had to jump ship – quite literally – in the middle of the Bristol Channel.

From there, we got a closer look at the weird landscape of the Gwent Levels as we headed towards the Usk estuary. The Levels, that coastal hinterland between second Severn Crossing and Newport, really do warrant that much over-used phrase, "a world apart". Protected from flooding by a mighty sea wall along its length, it's a forgotten corner of Wales that few people have heard of, let alone visited. It has a surreal, lost world quality, more reminiscent of the Fens or the Netherlands than Wales. The Gwent Levels anonymity is even more remarkable given their proximity to two of Wales' largest urban sprawls, Cardiff and Newport, and numerous outcrops of heavy industry, most dramatically the vast steel plant at Llanwern, whose billowing smokestacks provide the oddest of backdrops to such gentle scenery.

Llanwern steelworks standing sentinel over the Gwent Levels

Before long, we were scooting along the sea wall at Goldcliff, a name that dates from Roman times, when the cliffs here were indeed seen to contain a mineral that glinted beguilingly like gold. The cliffs are all gone now, replaced by the sea wall, but Goldcliff still clings to its past. We went ashore to meet Adrian Williams, the last registered putcher fisherman on the Severn, although even he is being paid not to fish for five years, in a maritime version of set-aside. Putcher fishing, unique to this little corner of the world, is done by erecting hundreds and hundreds of funnel-shaped putcher nets in a wooden rank below the high tide mark. The tide flows out, and salmon get caught in the nets, which are then emptied at low tide by Adrian. Even on a good catch, he'll only get a handful of fish.

The practice, Adrian told me, dates back to the time of Henry VIII in the sixteenth century. In one of those incredible examples of how the

British Establishment carved up the land and wealth for their own ends, Henry granted many of the lands hereabouts to Eton College, that extremely expensive and famous private school near Windsor, and, even to this day, some of the local farmers pay rent to Eton. The school licensed the putcher fishermen and regularly received payment both financial and in fish. As ever, it's not an arrangement that works both ways. No local lads have been sent on scholarships to Eton.

We also took in Goldcliff church, one of six hugely impressive parish churches that dominate the Gwent Levels. It's a lovely spot, surrounded by corn billowing in the summer breeze and a dark, tree-filled graveyard. There's a plaque in the church commemorating a huge flood in 1606, when the combination of one of the world's highest tides next to land as flat as a pancake combined to allow the sea to speed in at such a rate, the whole of the Gwent coastline was flooded and around 2,000 people were drowned. The plaque, however, has other things to commemorate:

> 1606. On the XX day of January
> Even as it came to pass the flud
> Did flow to the edge of this same
> Bras and in this parish theare was
> Lost 5000 and od pownds besides,
> XXII people was in this parish
> Drownd.

Great sense of proportion, there, that losing five grand took precedence over the loss of human life. Maybe it's the Eton effect.

The scenery became ever more urbanised as we neared the mouth of the river Usk, yr Afon Wysg. Dominating the horizon is the old Uskmouth power station, whose old dumping ground has undergone an amazing renaissance in recent years to become a wildlife reserve. The initial cash to develop the project came from the company behind the building of the controversial barrage just ten miles away at Cardiff Bay, and its aim was to provide the wading birds that were losing their mudflat habitat in the capital with a replacement. It seems to have worked to some extent, though it doesn't, personally, make me feel any more well disposed to the Cardiff scheme. To me, it smacks of man's arrogance when it comes to projects that aim to "conquer" nature. The old tidal habitat of Cardiff Bay had a real beauty of its own, but that wasn't good enough for the egotistical planners. They decreed that the only valid waterfront is a sterile artifical lake, so that's what we got. Nature, of course, has responded in the rising water tables of Grangetown and Butetown and in the swarm of flesh-hungry midges that flock to the waterside restaurants and bars every summer's evening.

Human arrogance threatens to overwhelm this area too in the proposals for a new Severnside Airport on the Gwent Levels, and even built out onto an artifical island in the Severn estuary. All that we'd seen over the previous few days was threatened by this outrageous plan, now backed by Sir Terry Matthews', usually named as "Wales' richest man" (despite living in Canada). Not content with building the monstrosity that is the Celtic Manor resort next to the M4 at Newport and attracting the 2010 Ryder Cup to it, Sir Terry now wants his own personal airport just down the road to fly his guests in to. Never mind that both Bristol and Cardiff International Airports are already within half an hour of the place. Never mind either that Severnside would destroy three thousand acres of wetland that is utterly unique in Wales. It was a relief to hear the plans turned down by the government in December 2003. Here's hoping they stay there.

The Uskmouth nature reserve, now under the aegis of the Countryside Council for Wales, is a wonderful addition to the area. Many migrating seabirds and wildfowl nest here, and, as we walked around, the crawks and squawks of the birds, hidden deep in reed-beds or flying elegantly overhead, were our constant companions. We hooked up with reserve warden Mike Mazzolini, whose route to his job has been, to say the least, unconventional. He'd worked in heavy industry for decades prior to coming here – his immediate previous job before Uskmouth was running a welding company in the building of the Millennium Stadium. Or, as he put, "I've spent thirty years polluting the atmosphere, and now I'm getting paid to try and save it." Mike is a local boy, who grew up on a farm on the Gwent Levels, and his passion and knowledge of the area was inspirational.

Mike took me on a wander along the foreshore, which was littered with debris of all kinds, from oil drums to railway sleepers, tree trunks to ropes. The power of the tide and the prevailing currents mean that everything in the Bristol Channel gets deposited on these shores, including the odd corpse from the bridges. There are two old lighthouses either side of the estuary. The one on the western side was, for a few years recently, a New Age retreat that specialised in pampering its guests with a bit of chakra-cleansing, aura re-balancing and the like. Well, who'd want to be seen with mucky chakras?

There's nothing very New Age about Newport as we glided into the mouth of the Usk estuary as the sun sank towards the horizon. Having only ever approached Newport by road, I'd been looking forward with curiosity to the short trip to the docks by boat. Docklands rarely show a city's best face and, let's be honest, Newport would never win many prizes in beauty contests. But there was a strange and surreal beauty to it that night, as we shimmied up the muddy waters of the Usk in the soft buttery light of a summer's evening. Boats bobbed in our wake and disused warehouses hunkered down on the shore. High on its funny, flared legs, the Transporter Bridge dominated the skyline like an overgrown kid's toy. All was silent, calm and very, very lovely. This was Newport, but not as we know it.

Thanks to the creation of its docks, Newport's population grew from just nine hundred to seventy thousand throughout the duration of the nineteenth century. It's still one of Britain's biggest docks, turning around half a million tonnes of steel a year for starters (though sadly, not steel produced at Llanwern, which now only processes stuff imported from other corners of the globe). We went to the docks and it's a mighty impressive operation. More than that, it was really heart-warming to see a docks that still is a docks, rather than having been tarted-up into a new marina, surrounded by yuppie bars and flats. There's not many left. Thanks to the rules of the docks, we were all kitted out in hard hats and high visibility jackets. Emyr filmed me walking along the dock edges dressed accordingly, and I felt unusually butch as I strode purposefully along. Suffice to say that when the episode was aired, virtually all of my mates told me afterwards that I looked like someone from a Village People tribute band.

Waiting for a bacon butty in Claire's Cabin, Newport Docks

While at the docks, we checked out the unofficial heart of the entire operation, the gloriously down-to-earth Claire's Cabin cafe that all the dockers end up in at some point. Claire and her business partner Lisa run the place with ruthless efficiency and endless good humour. Two good-looking young lasses let loose in the virtually all-male environment of the docks requires some balls, and Claire and Lisa have sure got them. Claire told me how they were, as she put, "one big happy family", even if she does end up acting as a shoulder to cry on, target practice for flirting or a surrogate mum most of the time.

No self-respecting docks would be complete without its traditional scrap metal merchants, these days re-named 'environmental cleansing operators' or the like, but Newport today really does lead the way in providing an environmentally sound solution to a global problem, namely that of disposing the harmful chloroflurocarbons (CFCs) in old fridges. Before 2001, units had to be sent abroad to have their noxious gases safely disposed of for re-cycling, but a new, state of the art recycling plant in Newport docks has begun turning the fridge mountain into a molehill.

When we were there, there were some thirty thousand dead fridges spread over a couple of acres, and more were arriving every day. It was an awesome and slightly surreal sight, and Emyr was in his element as he shot weird and wonderful angles on the rusting heaps. Good on Newport for throwing its lot in with these new industries, because, I couldn't help but think that if all those fridges were left to pile up in somewhere like London, they'd give it a fancy title and award it the Turner Prize.

Spend some time in Newport, and you can't help but draw inevitable comparisons with nearby booming Cardiff. Down in the Pillgwenlly area of town, normally known as plain old Pill, the contrasts are marked indeed, for this is the part of Newport most like the Cardiff Bay area. Like Cardiff Bay, Pill is the area that grew up to house those dependent on the docks for work. Like Cardiff Bay, Pill became Newport's multi-racial melting pot, where dozens of different cultures rub shoulders and have done for decades. But unlike Cardiff Bay, Pill has barely seen a penny of public money being invested in it, and the results – boarded-up shops, blanked-out pubs and so on – are there for all to see.

Upstream from Pill, adjacent to the city centre, you start to see where some of the money has been spent. A flash new arts centre is rising fast near Newport's dramatic sculptural homage to its industrial past, the Steel Wave. In 2002, a medieval ship was found as they dug the new centre's foundations, a sharp reminder of days gone by in a city that some see as a bit short on its sense of the past. Newport's castle, for instance, has got to be the most forlorn and miserably-sited in all of Wales. Hemmed in by a busy road, the mainline railway, a roundabout and the river, the castle looks like a reluctant guest at the wrong party.

Just over the river is perhaps the biggest recent success story in

Newport, in the shape of *TJ's* nightclub, erstwhile mecca of the nineties Welsh rock new wave. For an all-too-brief period of the 1990s, Newport was the recognised capital of rock cool. It was named as the "British Seattle", and for a short time, pony-tailed A&R executives from London would trot down to the city and sign up any group of lads who could twang a guitar convincingly enough. And *TJ's* was the epicentre of the scene. The Manic Street Preachers played there, in the days when they were still edgy and hungry, when they still had Richey and before they became the Welsh version of U2, churning out pompous stadium rock. Grunge god Kurt Cobain of Nirvana is said to have proposed to Courtney Love on the premises. And, even though the paint's peeling in *TJ's* and the A&R men have long since disappeared back to Soho, there's still a scene in Newport. For starters, I have never seen so many baggy-trousered wannabe skater punks as there were on the city's streets. It's all part of Newport's fast and furious charm.

It was a long overdue decision to make Newport a city, and it finally succeeded in 2002 as part of the Queen's Golden Jubilee celebrations. For the Jubilee, HRH was to grant city status to one town each from Wales, Scotland, England and Northern Ireland. Newport won the Welsh contest, Paisley the Scottish, Preston the English, but, depressingly true to form, things weren't so simple in Ulster. To avoid any taint of sectarian favouritism, two were chosen: Newry (a predominantly Catholic town) and Lisburn (predominantly Protestant). We were filming in Newport only a matter of months after the announcement had been made, and the biggest boom industry of the moment seemed to be converting any sign that said "town" to one declaring Newport's gleaming new city status. It was the right decision though, and I say that as someone loyal to my local hotspots of Machynlleth and Aberystwyth, both very much also-rans in the race.

Newport's magnificent Transporter Bridge

162

We saved the best of Newport to last. There are fifty-five Newports in the world, but only one has a Transporter Bridge. In this noisy, lively city, it's the perfect antidote, a beast that combines beauty with brawn. Shortly after the bridge opened in 1906, it was described with rare clarity by a local councillor as "a giant with the grace of Apollo and the strength of Hercules". And there is something very powerful about the bridge, its functional purpose mixed wonderfully with a mad fantasy quality, like something straight out of *Chitty Chitty Bang Bang* or from the drawing board of Heath Robinson. It takes a couple of minutes to crank the car platform across the muddy waters of the River Usk, swirling menacingly below. In this age of speedy transport it may all seem a little long-winded, but you could always recall the words of Newport's very own supertramp poet, W. H. Davies:

What is this life, if, full of care,
We have no time to stand and stare?

And the Newport Transporter Bridge is a fine place to do just that.

The day we filmed at the bridge, I must have been across it eight or nine times, in order to provide Emyr with the right amount of angles and views. But he was saving the worst for me, as he decided that he wanted to film from the top of the bridge, some two hundred feet up. We trudged up the couple of hundred steps in one of the bridge's splindly legs to the platform that ran across the top. It's just metal meshing, with nothing solid between you and the ground, and I wasn't faking the fear that was gripping me every time I tip-toed closer to the bridge's edge. There were marvellous views of the city and the river from there, however, and I had to admit – through gritted teeth – that it had been worth the climb and the nervous sweat. It was a very unconventional ending to a highly unconventional sea journey, but it was a hell of a lot of fun, and remains one of my personal highlights of *Coast to Coast*.

GLOSSARY
OF WELSH PLACE-NAMES

CHAPTER 1
Chester – *Caer* [abbrev. of
 Caerlleon Fawr]
river Dee – *Afon Dyfrdwy*
Connah's Quay – *Cei Connah*
Flintshire Bridge – *Pont Sir y Fflint*
Holywell – *Treffynnon*
Point of Ayr colliery – *Y Parlwr Du*
Offa's Dyke – *Clawdd Offa*
Deeside – *Glannau Dyfrdwy*
Buckley – *Bwcle*

CHAPTER 2
Colwyn Bay – *Bae Colwyn*
Rhos-on-Sea – *Llandrillo-yn-Rhos*
Little Orme – *Trwyn y Fuwch*
Great Orme – *Y Gogarth*
Anglesey – *Ynys Môn*
Puffin Island – *Ynys Seiriol*
Menai Strait – *Afon Menai*
Swellies – *Pwll Ceris*
Menai Bridge – *Porthaethwy*
Beaumaris – *Biwmares*

CHAPTER 3
Amlwch Port – *Porth Amlwch*
East Mouse – *Ynys Amlwch*
Middle Mouse – *Ynys Badrig*
West Mouse – *Maen y Bugail*
Cemaes Bay – *Cemais*
Holyhead – *Caergybi*
Dublin – *Dulyn*
Salt Island – *Ynys Halen*
Holy Island – *Ynys Cybi*
South Stack – *Ynys Lawd*
Giantess' Apron – *Barclodiad y Gawres*
Newborough – *Niwbwrch*

CHAPTER 4
Bardsey Island – *Ynys Enlli*
Bardsey Sound – *Swnt Enlli*
Cardigan Bay – *Bae Ceredigion*

CHAPTER 5
Black Rock Sands – *Morfa Bychan*
Shell Island – *Mochras (Ynys Fochras)*
Barmouth – *Abermo*
St Patrick's Causeway – *Sarn Badrig*

CHAPTER 6
Fairbourne – *Y Friog*
Bird Rock – *Craig Aderyn*

CHAPTER 7
Cardigan – *Aberteifi*
Cardigan Island – *Ynys Aberteifi*
New Quay – *Cei Newydd*

CHAPTER 8
St Justinian's – *Porth Stinan*
St David's Head – *Penmaen Dewi*
St Davids – *Tyddewi*
Pembrokeshire – *Sir Benfro*
Ramsey Island – *Ynys Dewi*
Strumble Head – *Pen Caer*
Fishguard – *Abergwaun*
Lower Fishguard – *Cwm*
Goodwick – *Wdig*

CHAPTER 9
Milford Haven – *Milffwrd*
St Bride's Bay – *Bae Sain Ffraid*
Newgale – *Niwgwl*
Solva – *Solfach*
Whitesands Bay – *Porth Mawr*

CHAPTER 10
Gower – *Penrhyn Gŵyr*
Swansea – *Abertawe*
Mumbles – *Y Mwmbwls*
Three Cliffs Bay – *Bae Tri Chlogwyn*
Worm's Head – *Pen Pyrod*
River Loughor – *Afon Llwchwr*

164

CHAPTER 11
Aberavon – *Aberafan*
Kenfig – *Cynffig*
Sker House – *Y Sgêr*
River Ogmore – *Afon Ogwr*
Nash Point – *Trwyn yr As*
Bristol Channel – *Môr Hafren*
Llantwit Major – *Llanilltud Fawr*
Vale of Glamorgan – *Bro Morgannwg*
Barry – *Y Barri*

CHAPTER 12
Chepstow – *Cas-gwent*
River Severn – *Afon Hafren*
River Wye – *Afon Gwy*
Gwent Levels – *Morfa Gwent*
Goldcliff – *Allteuryn*
River Usk – *Afon Wysg*
Cardiff Bay – *Bae Caerdydd*
Newport – *Casnewydd*